Composition:
models and exercises

Composition: models and exercises

DESMOND J. NUNAN
PHILIP McFARLAND

SECOND EDITION

JOHN E. WARRINER

General Editor

HARCOURT BRACE JOVANOVICH, INC.

New York   Chicago   San Francisco   Atlanta   Dallas

THE AUTHORS

DESMOND J. NUNAN taught English for twelve years in both public and private schools, served as Director of Curriculum in the West Chester (Pa.) Public Schools and, since 1966, has been Assistant to the Superintendent of Schools in the Allentown (Pa.) School District. He majored in English at Columbia College and received his doctorate from the University of Pennsylvania.

PHILIP McFARLAND has taught English for a number of years at Concord Academy, Concord, Massachusetts. Earlier he served as an editor in educational publishing. He is the author of the novel *A House Full of Women.*

GENERAL EDITOR

JOHN E. WARRINER has taught English for thirty-two years in junior and senior high schools and in college. He is the chief author of the *English Grammar and Composition* series and a coauthor of the *English Workshop* series.

ISBN   0–15–310979–3

ACKNOWLEDGMENTS: *For permission to reprint copyrighted material, grateful acknowledgment is made to the following publishers, authors, and agents:*

THOMAS E. ADAMS and THE SEWANEE REVIEW: From "Sled" by Thomas E. Adams from *The Sewanee Review,* Winter 1961, copyright © 1961 by the University of the South.
ATHENEUM HOUSE, INC.: From *A New England Reader* by Van Wyck Brooks, copyright © 1962 by Van Wyck Brooks.
BRANDT & BRANDT: From *The Forest* by Stewart Edward White, copyright 1903 by Doubleday & Company, Inc.
CHILTON BOOK COMPANY OF PHILADELPHIA AND NEW YORK: From *Empires in the Dust* by Robert Silverberg, copyright © 1963 by Robert Silverberg.
THOMAS Y. CROWELL COMPANY, INC. and METHUEN & COMPANY LIMITED: From *King Solomon's Ring* by Konrad Z. Lorenz, copyright © 1952 by Thomas Y. Crowell Company, New York, publishers.
DODD, MEAD & COMPANY: From *North with the Spring* by Edwin Way Teale, copyright 1951 by Edwin Way Teale.
DOUBLEDAY & COMPANY, INC.: From *This Hallowed Ground* by Bruce Catton, copyright © 1955, 1956 by Bruce Catton. From *Footnotes on Nature* by John Kieran, copyright 1947 by John Kieran.
E. P. DUTTON & COMPANY, INC., and LONGMANS, GREEN & COMPANY LIMITED: From the book *Ring of Bright Water* by Gavin Maxwell, copyright © 1960 by Gavin Maxwell. Published 1961 by E. P. Dutton & Co., Inc.
FABER AND FABER LIMITED: From *The Innocent Eye* by Herbert Read.
HARCOURT BRACE JOVANOVICH, INC.: From *The Human Comedy* by William Saroyan, copyright 1943 by William Saroyan. From *Davy Crockett* by Constance Rourke. From *Mama's Bank Account* by Kathryn Forbes, copyright 1943 by Kathryn Forbes. From

Contents

SECTION ONE: FINDING IDEAS

Lesson 1 **People and Places** 3

Model 1   Kathryn Forbes in *Mama's Bank Account*, 3

Model 2   John Kieran in *Footnotes on Nature*, 6

Lesson 2 **Your Experience** 10

Model 3   Daniel P. Mannix in *All Creatures Great and Small*, 10

Model 4   Walt Kelly in "Enterprise," 13

Lesson 3 **Your Interests** 17

Model 5   Konrad Z. Lorenz in *King Solomon's Ring*, 17

Model 6   Herbert S. Zim in *Plants*, 19

Lesson 4 **Your Opinions** 22

Model 7   R. P. Tristram Coffin in "A Patchwork Quilt," 22

Model 8   John W. Gardner in *Self-Renewal*, 24

SECTION TWO: THE PARAGRAPH

Lesson **5** **The Topic Sentence**   **31**

      Model 9   Marian Anderson in *My Lord, What a Morning*, 31

      Model 10   Antony Alpers in *Dolphins*, 32

      Model 11   Paul Gallico in "The Gentle Art of Swordplay," 33

Lesson **6** **Unity in Paragraphs**   **36**

      Model 12   Ruth Benedict in *Patterns of Culture*, 36

      Model 13   Franklyn M. Branley in *Exploration of the Moon*, 37

      Model 14   Gavin Maxwell in *Ring of Bright Water*, 38

Lesson **7** **Paragraph Development**   **41**

      DEVELOPING WITH EXAMPLES

      Model 15   Bruce Catton in *This Hallowed Ground*, 41

      Model 16   Edwin Way Teale in *North with the Spring*, 42

      DEVELOPING WITH AN INCIDENT

      Model 17   Stanley Kahan in *Introduction to Acting*, 44

      DEVELOPING WITH REASONS

      Model 18   George Barrow in *Your World in Motion*, 46

Lesson **8** **Coherence in Paragraphs** **48**

    CHRONOLOGICAL ORDER

    Model 19   Floyd L. Darrow in *Masters of Science and Invention,* 49

    ORDER OF IMPORTANCE

    Model 20   John L. Chapman in *Atlas: The Story of a Missile,* 51

    ORDER OF LOCATION

    Model 21   Gerald Durrell in *The Overloaded Ark,* 52

SECTION THREE: CHOOSING WORDS

Lesson **9** **Nouns** **57**

    Model 22   Clarence Day in *Life with Father,* 57
    Model 23   Marston Bates in *The Forest and the Sea,* 59
    Model 24   Cornelius Ryan in *June 6, 1944: The Longest Day,* 60

Lesson **10** **Adjectives** **63**

    Model 25   Louisa May Alcott in *Little Women,* 64
    Model 26   John Galsworthy in "The Apple Tree," 65

Lesson **11** **Verbs** **67**

    Model 27   Constance Rourke in *Davy Crockett,* 67
    Model 28   Peg Bracken in *The I Hate to Cook Book,* 69
    Model 29   Loren Eiseley in *The Immense Journey,* 70

Lesson **12** **Adverbs**   **72**

Model 30   Jack London in "All-Gold Canyon,"72
Model 31   Herman Melville in *Typee,* 75
Model 32   Thomas E. Adams in "Sled," 76

SECTION FOUR: DESCRIPTION

Lesson **13** **Using Specific Details**   **81**

Model 33   John Hersey in *A Single Pebble,* 81
Model 34   John A. Crow in *Mexico Today,* 83
Model 35   Willa Cather in *O Pioneers!,* 84

Lesson **14** **Showing the Location of Details**   **88**

Model 36   Robert Silverberg in *Empires in the Dust,* 89
Model 37   Herbert Read in *The Innocent Eye,* 90
Model 38   Nathaniel Hawthorne in "Dr. Heidegger's Experiment," 92

Lesson **15** **Using Sensory Details**   **95**

Model 39   Jesse Stuart in "Thanksgiving Hunter," 96
Model 40   Frank Bolles in "A Thunderstorm in the Forest," 96
Model 41   E. M. Forster in *A Passage to India,* 98

SECTION FIVE: NARRATION

Lesson **16** **Writing a Narrative**   **103**

Model 42   John Steinbeck in *Travels with Charley,* 104

Lesson **17** **Description in Narration**   **111**

   Model 43   D. H. Lawrence in "Adolf," 111

Lesson **18** **Using Dialogue**   **121**

   Model 44   William Saroyan in *The Human Comedy*, 121

SECTION SIX: EXPOSITION

Lesson **19** **Developing a Topic**   **133**

   Model 45   Pat Hunt in "Life Patterns of Baboons," 133

Lesson **20** **Explaining a Process**   **138**

   Model 46   Stewart Edward White in "On Making Camp," 138

Lesson **21** **Description in Exposition**   **143**

   Model 47   J. Y. Cousteau in *The Silent World*, 143

Lesson **22** **Narration in Exposition**   **147**

   Model 48   Leonard Hall in "Lively Adventures," 147

Lesson **23** **Supporting an Opinion**   **153**

   Model 49   James Michener in "Why I Like Japan," 153

Index of Writers   **157**

Index of Writing Skills   **159**

Finding Ideas

LESSON **1**
People and Places

When first assigned a composition, you may find one question particularly bothersome: "What shall I write about?" The opening section of this book helps you answer that question.

For one thing, you might write about people — about any of the many interesting people you know. Your friends, classmates, teachers, neighbors, members of your family, or anyone you have ever noticed and stopped to watch can provide the raw material for an effective composition.

In the following selection, Kathryn Forbes writes about her mother, who was born in Norway and later moved to the United States, where she became an American citizen.

1   **Kathryn Forbes in *Mama's Bank Account***

[1] In those days, if anyone had asked Mama unexpectedly, "What nationality are you?" I believe she would have answered without hesitation, "I am a San Franciscan."

[2] Then quickly, lest you tease her, she would add, "I mean Norvegian. American citizen."

[3] But her first statement would be the true one.

[4] Because from the moment she was to step off the ferryboat, confused and lonely in a strange

land, San Francisco was to become suddenly and uniquely her own.

[5] "Is like Norvay," the Aunts said Mama had declared.

[6] And straightway she'd taken the city to her heart.

[7] Mama learned so many things about San Francisco. She could tell you how to get to Telegraph Hill; what time the boats came in at Fisherman's Wharf; the names of the young boys who tended the steaming crab kettles along Bay Street; and where to find the blue and yellow lupins * at Land's End.

[8] The cable cars were an endless delight, and Mama's idea of a perfect Sunday afternoon was for Papa to take us riding on them from one transfer point to another.

[9] Papa would tell of the time Mama took out her citizenship papers and astounded the solemn court by suddenly reciting the names of the streets. "Turk, Eddy, Ellis, O'Farrel," Mama had said proudly, "Geary, Post, Sutter, Bush, and Pine."

[10] Papa said the clerk had quite a time making Mama understand that such knowledge was not necessary for citizenship.

[11] Mama made friends with an Armenian lady who had a store out on Third Street and gave her her best *lutefisk* ° recipe. Best of all, though, Mama liked to explore Chinatown. Old Sing Fat and Mama held long conversations over the counters of his Grant Avenue Bazaar. Like as not, she would come home to Castro Street with a tiny bag of lichee nuts † or preserved ginger. And if any of

* **lupins:** small flowers.
° *lutefisk:* fish soaked in lye water and then boiled.
† **lichee nuts:** the sweet fruit of the lichee tree, native to China.

us were ill in bed, Mama would go down and get us a small package of those Chinese water flowers that open into amazing beauty when dropped into water.

[12] And if anyone ever asked us where we were born, Mama instructed us, we should say "San Francisco." Didn't copies of our birth certificates, neatly framed and hung on the wall of Papa's and Mama's room, testify to that proud fact?

[13] "After all," Papa used to tease her, "after all, San Francisco isn't the *world*."

[14] But to Mama it was just that. The world.

The Writer's Craft

1. What would you say was the author's chief purpose in writing this selection? Was it to give the reader a clear picture of what Mama looked like? Was it to describe Mama's friends? Was it to tell about one of Mama's characteristics — her love of San Francisco? Give reasons for your answer.

2. What do paragraphs 7, 9–10, and 12 contribute to the main purpose of the selection?

3. Though most of the selection is concerned with Mama's feelings about San Francisco, several of her personality traits are touched upon. What is your general impression of her? Was she good-natured? friendly? cheerful? What does paragraph 8 reveal about her personality? What does the mention of her friendship with the Armenian lady and Sing Fat tell you about her?

Now You Try It

Write a composition of 150–200 words about a man or woman you know well. Don't try to include every detail about the person. Instead, choose no more than one or two outstanding characteristics, then make those characteristics clear to the reader. You will probably want to include incidents that reveal personality traits (his humor, his stubbornness, his friendliness, etc.). You may also want to quote remarks typical of the person, perhaps even some of the remarks other people make about him.

Places you have visited or lived in make good subjects to write about. In the model below, John Kieran, an American naturalist, recalls the farm where he spent his summers as a boy.

2   John Kieran in *Footnotes on Nature*

[1] When I was about eleven years old my father bought a forty-acre farm in Dutchess County, New York, to serve as a "summer place" for our family that included two parents, seven children, numerous cheerful relatives, and sundry pet stock such as dogs, cats, rabbits, and pigeons. The farmhouse was a rambling affair of twelve rooms with low ceilings and creaking floors.

[2] During our summers in Dutchess County I was rarely under a roof from June until September except for necessary attendance at such vital meetings as the family breakfasts, dinners, and suppers (with cookies and milk before going to bed) at the family table in the farmhouse. I roamed the fields and the woods the rest of the day, and at night I slept in a tent that was pitched on a little hill north of the farmhouse. On clear nights I would move my cot out of the tent and sleep on the open hillside under the moon and the stars.

[3] Out of the sky in the dark would come strange noises from invisible birds passing overhead. As I lay on my cot in the tent I thought them as hoarse as the raven that croaked the fatal en-

trance of Duncan under the battlements of Macbeth. I turned to the young farmer up the road for an explanation and he said the invisible birds were "quowks," but it was some years later in Van Cortlandt Park swamp in New York City that I first laid eyes on black-crowned night herons and recognized them as the owners and operators of those weird voices heard under the cover of darkness in Dutchess County.

[4] There were the other sounds to be heard in the eerie hush of summer nights. At midnight in my unguarded tent, I once heard what seemed like the sound of slow footfalls in the dead leaves that carpeted the ground in a black locust grove near my tent. Certainly something was walking or moving about at short intervals there in the darkness. I slipped quietly from my cot to investigate. As I approached it, the sound ceased. When I went off a bit, the sound of half-shuffling footsteps began again. Ultimately I tracked down the culprit. It was a toad on a night prowl.

[5] One season we had stunning sound effects in our little valley. A family of red foxes grew up on the hillside opposite my tent, and they used to "squall" at night around an old red barn, probably because there were chickens and turkeys roosting in the barn and on the low branches of trees around it. This "squalling" is unearthly —almost demoniac * — in quality.

[6] But best of all summer sounds I loved the baying of the hounds on the trail of some rabbit or fox in the night. Many times, on hearing the hounds running in the moonlight, I would dress myself, no matter what the hour, and go off to be near the chase. Often I sat for hours on a hilltop,

* **demoniac:** devilish.

listening to the music of the hounds floating up from the dim valley in the deep quiet of a moon-lit night.

The Writer's Craft

1. The author begins with a few facts about the farm, its inhabitants, and his life there. Then he uses paragraphs 3–6 to convey his chief impression of the farm. Which of the five senses does he appeal to most in those paragraphs?

2. Some of the sounds are described so vividly that the reader can almost hear them. Paragraph 4, for example, describes the sound of a toad on a night prowl. What did the toad sound like?

3. Which summer sound did the author like best? Why does he mention that particular sound where he does in the model?

Now You Try It

Select one of the following assignments:

1. Write a brief composition describing your home in a way that emphasizes the sounds heard there. The familiar hum of the refrigerator, the blare of a television or radio, the comforting noises of dinner being prepared — those and other sounds can be combined to create a single clear impression. Through your writing, you may wish to present your home as a warm and comfortable place in which to live or, perhaps, as a somewhat monotonous or rather noisy and hectic place. Select details that support whatever impression you want to convey.

2. Choose a familiar place — your classroom, the school cafeteria, a neighborhood store — and write a description of it. Before you begin the composition, make a list of the objects that you will include to create a clear impression of the place, and list the sights, sounds, or smells you associate with those objects. If one object is more important than the others, save that one for the end of the composition.

3. Choose a favorite place — a beach, a park, an attic — and write a short description of it. Describe its most vivid sights, sounds, and smells. In doing so, try to create a strong overall impression of the place so that the reader will understand why you are fond of it.

....

Remember

- *People and places make good subjects for a composition.*
- *In writing about people and places, emphasize outstanding characteristics.*
- *In writing about a place, include distinctive sights, sounds, and smells associated with it.*

LESSON **2**

Your Experience

Everyone has had experiences that would make good subjects for compositions. Think back over all the amusing or surprising things in which you have taken part; there must be several you would enjoy writing about. The trick is to stop searching for an incident that is unique, startling, or sensational. The experience that will interest your reader most is the one that interests *you* most, even if it is as ordinary as the first time you went swimming or the time a substitute teacher took over your class.

The two models in this lesson are based on experiences that happened to their authors. First, read the selection by Daniel P. Mannix, which tells of his experiences with a pet raccoon named Wayatcha.

3 **Daniel P. Mannix**
    in *All Creatures Great and Small*

[1] I got Wayatcha when he was still a baby from a grocer who found him one morning in the storeroom. Wayatcha had gotten his head stuck in a jar of applesauce and couldn't get it out again. I took the baby to the loft of our garage-barn and tried to get the jar loose. There has been a great deal written about the marvel- 5

ous manner in which animals know when you are trying to help them. I've never noticed it. I have yet to see one you didn't have to hog-tie [10] before lancing an abscess or washing out a cut, and Wayatcha was no exception. After struggling with him for half an hour and getting badly scratched, I finally had to break the jar. Wayatcha suffered no ill effects from his experience [15] except a terrible bellyache from eating too much applesauce. I spent the next week trying to overcome the little wild creature's timid nature and another two years trying to put the fear of God into him. [20]

[2] Wayatcha tamed quickly — partly because he was young, but mainly because he was lonely. Raccoons stay with their mothers for at least a year after they are born, and I can only suppose that Wayatcha's mother had been killed, forc- [25] ing the baby to shift for himself. At first he had a hard time understanding how anyone who had treated him so badly (he clearly regarded my efforts to get the jar off his head as a brutal attack) should now be bringing him food. After much [30] mental agony, he managed to take cookies from my hand, although he snarled and ran if I tried to touch him. But he didn't really lose his fear of me until I tried to play a joke on him.

[3] One afternoon while Wayatcha was sit- [35] ting on the barn floor beside me eating cookies, I held out a handful of raisins with my fist closed. Wayatcha finished the cookies and waddled over to inspect my fist. He smelled it, located the raisins, and then tried to pry my fingers open with [40] his little black paws. When this did not work, he patted my hand and looked up questioningly. I chuckled to myself and said nothing. Then Wayatcha sat down with my fist in his lap to think it over. [45]

[4] Raccoons are very fond of clams; they open them by a sharp bite at the joint. I had forgotten this trick but Wayatcha had not. A few minutes later he had the raisins and I was getting first aid from a bottle of iodine. That was the [50] end of Wayatcha's backwardness. After that he thought nothing of taking a flying leap at me as soon as I opened the cage door and hanging onto my necktie with one hand while he went through my pockets with the other. If I had known more [55] about animals, I would then and there have begun to discipline Wayatcha.

The Writer's Craft

1. You can tell that Daniel Mannix is genuinely interested in the experience he is writing about. Notice, for example, how he accounts for everything that happened. In paragraph 2, how does he account for Wayatcha's being alone although the raccoon was still a baby? In paragraph 4, how does he account for Wayatcha's method of getting the raisins from his closed fist?

2. In paragraph 2 the author writes that Wayatcha "clearly regarded my efforts to get the jar off his head as a brutal attack." The statement is amusing because the raccoon is being referred to as though it were a human being. Find two other places in the selection where the author uses that same device again.

3. Do you think the author succeeds in conveying Wayatcha's personality to the reader? Mention several of the raccoon's personality traits that you discovered from reading the selection.

4. So vividly is the experience described that the reader, besides getting to know Wayatcha, begins to know the author, too — another important reason why the selection makes good reading. What specifically does the selection reveal about Daniel Mannix? Do you think he is patient or impatient? Is he kind? Is he good-natured? Explain your answers.

Your experiences with animals, especially your own or other people's pets, can provide topics for effective compositions. Even if you or your friends do not own a pet, the recollection of a walk through a park or a trip to a zoo or farm will suggest animal subjects to write about.

Write a composition based on your experience with an animal. You might choose to write about a pleasant experience (getting a kitten for Christmas), a painful experience (being bitten by a stray dog), or a surprising experience (finding frogs in your bed at camp). Your composition should be about 150–200 words long.

The opening paragraph might well set the stage for your experience and tell when and where it took place. Do not try to include too many incidents; one or two interesting events related in some detail are better than a whole string of unimportant ones told very generally. Finally, remember to describe what happened as vividly and accurately as possible. If you can get something of the animal's personality across to your reader, so much the better.

In the next selection Walt Kelly, creator of the comic-strip character Pogo, tells about a boyhood undertaking. In doing so, he makes a rather simple, everyday experience both interesting and amusing.

4 Walt Kelly in "Enterprise"

[1] Cranberry Campbell, Binney Robertson, and I started an outdoor candle factory one time. We dug a hole in the backyard and built a fire in it, then laid a piece of metal screening over the flames and placed a pot on that. Into the pot we put pieces of paraffin filched from our mothers. (They used paraffin to seal the jars of homemade jellies, jams, peach preserves, and cooked string beans that la-

dies in those days prepared during the summer.) After the paraffin was melted, we poured it into a short piece of pipe which had a string stretched through its interior, and when the stuff cooled we had a candle, or so we considered it — sometimes with a few ants imbedded in the dirty wax and with smoky stripes giving it a kind of glum decoration.

[2] Getting the candle out of its mold posed a problem at first, but American know-how in the person of Binney Robertson, the inventor, showed us how to heat the outside of the pipe and pull the wax monstrosity out by its string. True, we pulled a lot of strings right out of the candles, but Robertson invented a system for rethreading the wick.

[3] We peddled the candles around the neighborhood at five cents each, starting out that morning with high hopes and ten candles and figuring what we would do with the fifty cents we were sure to get. Most of the mothers looked at the candles with distinct distaste and at noon we still had ten. So we declared a fire sale and slashed the price to two cents each. Asked why it was a fire sale, we truthfully replied that the goods were a little damaged by smoke. "Also by ants," said Mrs. Knott as she bought two.

[4] Mrs. Campbell and my mother were having coffee in our kitchen when we approached with the reduction in price. Cranberry explained to his mother that this was her chance to snap up the remaining eight. I pointed out that they were handmade and therefore worth a great deal more than store candles, which at the time were selling at two for a nickel. We described how much more valuable the wax was now than in its original form, but my mother put an end to the pitch by trying one of the candles. It burned with a sputtering blue and dismal flame for about three seconds and finally

wilted, leaned gently sideways, and went out. We left, closing the screen door as quietly and as quickly as we could.

[5] Cranberry suggested that we should try all the candles down in the cellar and sell only those that were guaranteed to stay lighted. Not one did, and in addition, they smelled pretty bad. We decided to try chewing them. But even this attempt at salvage was no good. They tasted pretty bad, too.

The Writer's Craft

1. Like the author of Model 3, the author of this selection seems genuinely interested in the experience he is relating. In paragraphs 1 and 2, for example, notice how thoroughly he explains the process of making candles. How did the boys melt the paraffin? How did they make the wicks? Do these details make the selection more interesting? In other words, in place of the detailed explanation in paragraphs 1 and 2, suppose that the author had written simply: "One time we figured out a way to make our own candles." If he had then continued with paragraph 3, not having told how the candles were made, would the rest of the passage have been as interesting as it is? Explain your answer.

2. Paragraphs 3 and 4 vividly describe the boys' attempts to sell their candles. Again, notice how many different details of the experience are explained. Why did the boys declare a fire sale? Why did they claim that their candles were worth more than store candles? What happened when Mrs. Kelly lighted one of the candles?

3. The author makes this experience seem funny — in part by remembering exactly how he felt at the time and by telling just what happened, even when such honesty makes him look slightly ridiculous. Notice, for example, his amusing description of the boys' exit at the end of paragraph 4: "We

left, closing the screen door as quietly and as quickly as we could." What is amusing about paragraph 5? What other parts of the selection did you find humorous?

Now You Try It

Select one of the following assignments:

1. No doubt you have gone into business at least once. Perhaps you set up a lemonade stand, or collected newspapers for the junkyard, or sold fudge, or shoveled snow, or baby-sat, or mowed lawns. As you remember your experience, does it seem funny? Write a brief composition in which you describe in detail your experience in business, telling what happened as amusingly as you can.

2. If you have never tried going into business, you have undoubtedly had other experiences with your friends or family that you would enjoy telling about. Choose one such interesting experience — a humorous one if possible — and write about it in a brief composition. Try to remember and describe exactly how you felt during the experience.

· ·

Remember

— *Your experiences can make good subjects for compositions.*

— *In describing an experience, tell what happened vividly and accurately.*

— *Let your reader know how you felt while the experience was in progress.*

LESSON **3**

Your Interests

Your interests make especially good subjects to write about. A hobby — building ship models, collecting stamps — can be used as the basis of a composition. A favorite sport that you enjoy discussing you will probably enjoy writing about, too. If you have been reading up on one of your interests — space exploration, animal training, cooking, sports cars — you can use your knowledge for an effective composition.

In the model below, a famous naturalist describes one of his interests.

5 **Konrad Z. Lorenz in _King Solomon's Ring_**

An aquarium costs almost nothing and is indeed wonderful. Cover the bottom of a glass tank with clean sand, and insert in this foundation a few stalks of ordinary water plants. Carefully pour in a few pints of tap water, and stand the whole thing on a sunny windowsill. As soon as the water has cleared and the plants have begun to grow, put in some little fish, or, better still, go with a jam jar and a small net to the nearest pond and draw the net a few times through the depth of the pool; you will have a myriad * of interesting organisms.

The whole charm of childhood still lingers, for me, in such a fishing net. This should, preferably,

* **myriad:** a vast number.

not be a complicated contraption with brass rim and gauze bag, but, according to Altenbergian tradition,* should rather be homemade in a matter of ten minutes: the rim an ordinary bent wire; the net a stocking, a piece of curtain, or a baby's napkin. With such an instrument, I caught, at the age of nine, the first Daphnia ° for my fish, thereby discovering the wonderworld of the fresh-water pond which immediately drew me under its spell. In the train of the fishing net came the magnifying glass; after this again a modest little microscope, and therewith my fate was sealed; for he who has once seen the intimate beauty of nature cannot tear himself away from it again. He must become either a poet or a naturalist and, if his eyes are good and his powers of observation sharp enough, he may well become both.

So you skim with your net through the water plants in the pond, generally filling your shoes with water and mud in the process. If you have chosen the right pond and found a place where "something is up," the bottom of the net will soon be swarming with glassily transparent, wriggling creatures. Tip up the base of the net and wash it out in the jam jar which you have already filled with water. When you arrive home, empty your catch carefully into the aquarium and contemplate the tiny world unfolding its secrets before your eyes.

* **Altenbergian tradition:** custom in Altenberg, the district in Austria where the writer lived.
° **Daphnia:** small water fleas used to feed fish.

The Writer's Craft

1. Setting up an aquarium is something the author of this selection has actually done. Where is that fact made clear? That Lorenz is writing from firsthand experience strengthens his account. How?

2. Obviously the author is enthusiastic about aquariums. Does his attitude increase the effectiveness of his writing? Explain.

3. The reader is furnished instructions on how to set up an aquarium for himself. Why is the selection more interesting than the usual instruction booklet?

The writer of Model 6 is interested in wood. In the selection, he reports on what he has learned about wood from reading and from talking with wood experts and lumbermen.

6   Herbert S. Zim in *Plants*

[1] It would not take a wood expert more than ten minutes to convince anyone that wood is the most fascinating and unique product in the whole plant kingdom. And he has some reasons for this. An expert can tell from a sample of wood more facts than you would ever dream possible. In most trees a ring is produced with each year's growth. Counting the rings gives you the age of the tree. In the western part of this country, where growth is closely tied up to rainfall, the width of the ring may be an accurate measure of the rainfall and climate that year. By counting backward through the rings, if you know the date the tree was cut, you can get a good picture of the climate even before the region was settled. It was through tree rings that scientists were able to fix the date of the great drought (1276–1300) in the Southwest that drove most of the Indian tribes to seek new places to live. The ring pattern of one tree can be tied to that of another, and it is even possible to match tree rings in an old piece of roof timber and thus tell the age of Indian ruins or other prehistoric buildings. Occasionally even ashes and bits of

charred wood from burned houses show enough tree rings so that their age can be worked out by matching with rings whose dates are known.

[2] If you're interested in the present instead of the past, wood can still be of great interest. The grain, pores, and wood cells that you can examine in detail with a magnifying glass vary from species to species. The density of wood varies from balsa at eight pounds per cubic foot to the hard, heavy, black ironwood that weighs sixty-seven pounds per cubic foot, and which sinks even when completely dry. Each kind of the more important woods has been found especially suited for some particular use: basswood for piano keys and slats in Venetian blinds; hickory for clothespins, ax handles, and ladders; dogwood for engraving blocks; locust for posts and fences. Many species find wide use in furniture construction, shipbuilding, and toymaking. The character of each kind of wood becomes so clear to the person who studies it that he can recognize a scrap of wood as easily as other people recognize a whole tree. It was such expert knowledge of wood that provided the most important clue in the famous Lindbergh kidnapping case of 1932. A homemade ladder was found at the scene of the crime and the wood expert, by comparing the structure of the wood in the ladder with scraps in a suspect's garage, was able to show that it was made from boards belonging to the suspect.

The Writer's Craft

1. The first sentence states that a wood expert considers wood "the most fascinating and unique product in the whole plant kingdom." The previous selection (Model 5) begins, "An aquarium . . . is indeed wonderful." In what ways are the openings of these two models similar? Do they both clearly express an attitude or opinion?

2. Why is an opening that expresses an attitude more interesting than one like the following: "In this composition I shall discuss wood"? When a writer begins by expressing an attitude, how will that attitude affect the rest of his composition?

3. The author provides a great deal of specific information to explain why wood is fascinating. Paragraph 1, for example, carefully explains ring patterns and the various facts that experts can learn from them. How do the rings in a sample of wood indicate the age of the tree? What else can experts learn from ring patterns? Find at least two other places in the selection where the author gives specific information to make his explanation clear.

4. Information is most interesting when it has some practical uses. What example is given in paragraph 2 to show how an expert's knowledge of wood can be put to practical use?

Now You Try It

Choose one of your hobbies, favorite activities, or principal interests to write about in a brief composition. Be sure the subject you choose is one with which you are quite familiar and in which you are genuinely interested. From the beginning of the composition make it clear to your reader exactly how you feel about your subject. If the composition includes directions on how to do something, make them simple and clear. And give specific information that will let your reader know just what you find interesting about your subject.

· ·

Remember

- *Your interests make good subjects for composition.*
- *A composition based on an interest should make the reader feel your enthusiasm for that interest.*
- *Your composition should contain specific information and clear explanations.*

LESSON **4**

Your Opinions

Your opinions can form the basis for effective compositions. Of course, in a composition it is not enough merely to state the opinion. That much you can do in a single sentence. To write a composition, you must include your reasons for believing as you do. Accordingly, only those opinions of yours on subjects about which you are reasonably well informed will be useful as composition topics.

In the following selection, R. P. Tristram Coffin gives his opinion of Maine cooking. Although that opinion is stated in the final sentence, long before then you know exactly what he thinks of Maine cooking — and why.

7   R. P. Tristram Coffin in "A Patchwork Quilt"

Good cooking is the universal sign of a civilization. If you can find a place where smelts * are baked with pork scraps crisscrossing them into a sheet of golden eloquence that makes a man forget his taxes are due, then you are in the midst of culture. The only real baked beans in Christendom never got south of the Kennebec. I shan't tell what

* **smelts:** small silvery fish.

goes into the pot besides beans, because I think the Kennebec has done enough for America already. Our smothered eels are no dish to be sneezed at. Baked raccoon is no poor man's meat. Nor are skates' fins. Lucullus' * mouth would water at them. We cook a deep apple pie in an iron skillet, with pork in it, that is a whole banquet in itself. And we have a chicken soup, with the whole chicken in it, and dumplings that are like thin sheets of the Promised Land. They are native things which the foreign macaroni is a poor mockery of. We have cod-lead dumplings, too, for sinkers in stouter stews, named for their shape, not their weight. We have hog's head cheese and calf's head cheese that beats the Pennsylvania Dutch. We used to have hulled corn which was as near heaven as maize could come. The Kennebec cod's head chowder can renew anybody's taste in life. And our flapjacks outdo the most aristocratic of southern waffles. They can, as Cap'n Bibber ° says, put whiskers on a man's feet. If you haven't eaten venison grilled over Maine spruce boughs in the frosty Maine air, then you have not started living. We have pies, of course, of all the New England varieties. But no pie on earth can come within a hundred miles of a Maine blueberry one with the spice and the sunshine of Maine boiling over its edges in the oven. And there is no real piecrust south of Portsmouth. By the test of cookery, Maine stands at the head of the nation.

* **Lucullus:** a Roman general famous for his banquets.
° **Cap'n Bibber:** a Maine fisherman, philosopher, and wit.

The Writer's Craft

1. In support of his opinion, the author mentions more than a dozen dishes that he says are cooked best in Maine. Do you think he needed to name so many different foods?

Suppose he had mentioned only two or three foods before stating his opinion: "By the test of cookery, Maine stands at the head of the nation." In that case would the opinion be as effectively supported as it is in the model?

2. When expressing such purely personal opinions as this one, writers often exaggerate — a device that can be very effective if the subject is not entirely serious. An example occurs in the second sentence of the selection. Smelts baked with pork scraps, even in Maine, don't really cause a man to forget that his taxes are due. Find two other statements in the model that strike you as exaggerations. Would they be as effective if the author had not exaggerated? Illustrate your answer by restating his points without exaggerating them.

3. Do you think the author's main purpose in writing this passage was to convince his readers that Maine cooking is the best in the nation? Do you think he was primarily concerned with describing Maine cooking and letting the reader know that it is excellent? Explain.

The following model develops an opinion (with which some readers may disagree) that adults — or many of them, at least — learn less than young people.

8 John W. Gardner in *Self-Renewal*

One of the reasons why mature people are apt to learn less than young people is that they are willing to risk less. Learning is a risky business, and they do not like failure. In infancy, when the child is learning at a truly phenomenal rate — a rate he will never again achieve — he is also experiencing a shattering number of failures. Watch him. See the innumerable things he tries and fails. And see how little the failures discourage him. With each year that passes he will be less blithe * about failure.

* **blithe:** carefree, happy.

By adolescence the willingness of young people to risk failure has diminished greatly. And all too often parents push them further along that road by instilling fear, by punishing failure or by making success seem too precious. By middle age most of us carry in our heads a tremendous catalogue of things we have no intention of trying again because we tried them once and failed — or tried them once and did less well than our self-esteem demanded.

One of the virtues of formal schooling is that it requires the student to test himself in a great variety of activities that are not of his own choosing. But the adult can usually select the kinds of activity on which he allows himself to be tested, and he takes full advantage of that freedom of choice. He tends increasingly to confine himself to the things he does well and to avoid the things in which he has failed or has never tried.

We pay a heavy price for our fear of failure. It is a powerful obstacle to growth. It assures the progressive narrowing of the personality and prevents exploration and experimentation. There is no learning without some difficulty and fumbling. If you want to keep on learning, you must keep on risking failure — all your life. It's as simple as that.

The Writer's Craft

1. In the author's opinion, mature people are apt to learn less than young people. Why? What examples of different attitudes toward failure does he include in his first paragraph?

2. Some parents, according to Gardner, push young people in adolescence "further along that road." Along what road? By what three means do the parents push them? What is the author's opinion of those parents? What phrase reveals that opinion?

3. The selection suggests a merit of formal schooling that you may not have thought of in just this way. What is that merit, or virtue? What fate, according to the author, overtakes many people after they finish school?

4. To what does "It" at the beginning of the second and third sentences of paragraph 3 refer? What opinion does the author express as his conclusion? Have the preceding paragraphs persuaded you that his conclusion is justified?

5. Compare this model with Model 7. Do you think John W. Gardner is more concerned than R. P. Tristram Coffin with convincing the reader to accept the opinion he holds? Explain your answer.

Now You Try It

Write a brief composition that supports one of your opinions. Before beginning the composition, state the opinion in a single clear sentence. Would that sentence be more effective at the beginning or at the end of the composition? Support your opinion with reasons. Incidentally, if your main purpose in writing the composition is a serious one — if it is actually to convince the reader that you are right — many of your reasons are likely to be facts. Discrimination, for example, may seem wrong in your opinion because — and this is a fact — more than one out of every ten American citizens is thereby treated differently from his fellows.

If you like, you may develop one of the following statements of opinion:

a. Report cards are unnecessary.
b. Summer is the best of the four seasons.
c. What I like least about city living is _____.
d. In general, commercials are the liveliest part of television.
e. _____ is the most important subject we study in school.
f. Better to try and fail than fail to try.

· ·

Remember

— *Your opinions can make good subjects for composition.*
— *An opinion should be clearly stated in a single sentence at the beginning or end of a composition.*
— *Support an opinion by giving your reasons for holding it.*

The Paragraph

LESSON **5**

The Topic Sentence

Very often a single sentence expresses the main idea of an entire paragraph. This *topic sentence,* as it is called, must obviously be composed with care, whether it occurs at the beginning, in the middle, or at the end of a paragraph. When placed at the beginning, it will tell the reader what the rest of the paragraph is about. In the following paragraph the topic sentence is placed at the beginning.

9   **Marian Anderson in *My Lord, What a Morning***

Life with Mother and Father, while he lived, was a thing of great joy, as I remember it now. It is easy to look back self-indulgently, feeling pleasantly sorry for oneself and saying I didn't have this and I didn't have that. But that is only the grown woman regretting the hardships of a little girl who never thought they were hardships at all. Certainly there were a lot of things she did not have, but she never missed them, because she didn't really need them. She had the things that really mattered.

1. The paragraph contains five sentences. Do each of the four after the first have something to do with the topic sentence, with which the paragraph opens?

2. Reread the paragraph. Then without looking back, state the topic of the paragraph in a single sentence. How close does your sentence come to the author's topic sentence?

3. Now read Model 9 as it appears below with a different opening sentence.

> *Recalling my childhood, I remember that I sang in a church choir.* It is easy to look back self-indulgently, feeling pleasantly sorry for oneself and saying I didn't have this and I didn't have that. But that is only the grown woman regretting the hardships of a little girl who never thought they were hardships at all. Certainly there were a lot of things she did not have, but she never missed them, because she didn't really need them. She had the things that really mattered.

Why is the italicized sentence a poor topic sentence for the paragraph? Does it tell what the whole paragraph is about?

Find the topic sentence in the paragraph below.

10   **Antony Alpers in *Dolphins***

Being gregarious * animals, dolphins live in a herd, and at times of danger they act as a herd, usually with the biggest male as leader. At Marineland, if something happens that disturbs the dolphins, such as the arrival of a newly captured shark, or any unfamiliar object, they will all bunch together and begin swimming in tight formation, with the youngest and their mothers in the middle. At such moments any little differences between them are forgotten. The bull forgets his annoyance

* **gregarious:** sociable; living in groups.

of a few moments before with the cheeky youngsters, the females forget their jealousies, and all become united, the bull determining what they do.
Usually they all swim round for a time, craning
their necks toward whatever it is that has fright-
ened them, keeping together and alert. In the open
sea no doubt the school either combines to attack
an enemy or makes off, according to what the
leader does. But the school itself is also its own de-
fense, simply by being together in one place.

The Writer's Craft

1. Which sentence states the controlling idea of the paragraph? In other words, which is the topic sentence?
2. Reread Model 10, substituting for the first sentence the
following:

> In times of danger the youngest dolphins and their
> mothers swim in the middle of the herd.

Would the statement above be broad enough as a topic sentence to cover all the points made in the paragraph? That is,
does the paragraph deal only with the youngest dolphins and
their mothers?

Sometimes a writer reserves his topic sentence for
the end of the paragraph. In the paragraph below, for
instance, Paul Gallico leads up to the topic sentence.

11 Paul Gallico in "The Gentle Art of Swordplay"

In boxing you feint * with foot, head, or hand.
You do the same in fencing. In a fight you take the
initiative, moving in with leads, or backpedal and
wait for a chance to counter. The same holds for a
sword fight. With gloves you try to block an oppo-

* **feint:** make a movement to divert attention from the real
attack.

nent's lead or jab. With a weapon this is called a parry. And in the ring, having nullified your opponent's lead with a block, you try to knock his head off with a timed counterpunch. Fencers call the same thing a riposte. The purpose of both games is to hit without being hit in return.

The Writer's Craft

1. Does the topic sentence — the last sentence — state the controlling idea of the whole paragraph? What is that controlling idea?

2. Suppose the author had chosen to put the topic sentence first in the paragraph. What change would have been necessary in the wording of the sentence? Rewrite the sentence so that it could be placed at the beginning. Then, using your revised wording, read the altered paragraph through. Are the effects of putting the topic sentence at the beginning and at the end different? Explain.

Now You Try It

1. Write a clear topic sentence, making a statement about one of the subjects listed below or about a subject of your own choosing. Be sure your topic sentence is neither too broad nor too narrow, and that it expresses an idea you can develop in a single paragraph.

a. The student council
b. Families
c. Violence
d. Thunderstorms
e. Parties
f. Space flights

When satisfied with your topic sentence, decide whether it would be more effective at the beginning or at the end of a paragraph. Remember that a topic sentence at the beginning puts the main idea of the paragraph immediately before the reader's eye. A topic sentence at the end serves more as a summary or conclusion to the paragraph.

2. Develop your topic sentence in a brief paragraph.

Remember

- *A topic sentence expresses the central idea of a paragraph.*
- *Although the topic sentence may appear anywhere within a paragraph, it often occurs at the beginning.*

LESSON

Unity in Paragraphs

A good paragraph is unified. That is, every sentence in the paragraph works toward the same goal — for example, toward developing a single idea. No matter how interesting or informative they may be, unrelated sentences do not appear in a unified paragraph.

Decide whether all the sentences in the paragraph below work toward the same goal.

12   Ruth Benedict in *Patterns of Culture*

The Pueblo Indians of the Southwest are one of the most widely known primitive peoples in Western civilization. They live in the midst of America, within easy reach of any transcontinental traveler. And they are living after the old native fashion. Their culture has not disintegrated like that of all the Indian communities outside of Arizona and New Mexico. Month by month and year by year, the old dances of the gods are danced in their stone villages, life follows essentially the old routines, and what they have taken from our civilization they have remodeled and subordinated to their own attitudes.

1. The first sentence states that the Pueblo Indians are one of the most widely known primitive peoples in Western civilization. The second sentence helps explain why they are so widely known. What reason does the sentence imply?

2. Does the remainder of the paragraph contribute further support to the topic sentence? In other words, do the remaining sentences help account for why the Pueblo Indians are regarded as primitive on the one hand, and why they are widely known on the other?

3. Is the paragraph unified?

The paragraph below is about buildings that colonists may someday construct on the moon. Again, as you read, consider whether the paragraph is unified.

13 Franklyn M. Branley
in *Exploration of the Moon*

Because the force of gravity on the moon is only one sixth that of the earth, entirely new structural concepts are possible. The major support of lunar buildings will probably be provided by sealing them and pumping them full of air under pressure. Broad expanses of Quonset-hut *-type buildings may be used, tied together with tunnels and divided into compartments to reduce the hazards of blowouts. Also, because of the lower gravity, it will be easier to circulate gases and liquids throughout the building, an important factor for the lunar architect to consider when designing installations for heat, power, sewage, and ventilation. Ramps and stairways can be much steeper because a man will be able to lift himself with only one sixth the effort normally required.

* **Quonset hut:** a long metal structure with a curved roof.

1. The topic sentence states that the slight force of gravity on the moon makes possible "entirely new structural concepts." Does the author go on to develop that idea in the rest of the paragraph?

2. Is there any sentence in the paragraph that strays from the central idea — that does *not* work toward supporting the topic sentence? Would you say that the paragraph is unified?

Here is another paragraph to consider for unity.

14 Gavin Maxwell in *Ring of Bright Water*

Otters are extremely bad at doing nothing. That is to say that they cannot, as a dog does, lie still and awake; they are either asleep or entirely absorbed in play or other activity. If there is no acceptable toy, or if they are in a mood of frustration, they will, apparently with the utmost good humor, set about laying the land waste. There is, I am convinced, something positively provoking to an otter about order and tidiness in any form, and the greater the state of confusion that they can create about them the more contented they feel. A room is not properly habitable to them until they have turned everything upside down; cushions must be thrown to the floor from sofas and armchairs, books pulled out of bookcases, wastepaper baskets overturned and the rubbish spread as widely as possible, drawers opened and contents shoveled out and scattered. The appearance of such a room where an otter has been given free rein resembles nothing so much as the aftermath of a burglar's hurried search for some minute * and valuable ob-

* **minute:** (mĭ·nōōt′) very small.

ject that he has believed to be hidden. I had never really appreciated the meaning of the word ransacked until I saw what an otter could do in this way.

The Writer's Craft

1. Otters, as you no doubt know, are appealing little animals that rather resemble beavers. What idea does the author express in the topic sentence of this paragraph about otters? In order to make it absolutely clear, he rephrases that idea. Where? Do the other sentences in the paragraph develop and illustrate the idea? Is the paragraph unified?

2. Could the sentence below be added to Model 14 without destroying the unity of the paragraph? Explain your answer.

> When sleeping, an otter often assumes the expression of tightly shut concentration that very small babies wear in sleep.

Now You Try It

1. Write a unified paragraph of approximately five sentences, developing one of the following topic sentences or a topic sentence of your own choosing.

a. Silence is rare in the city.
b. Schools of the future will be vastly different from those of today.
c. Most plants need sunlight.
d. America's history is unique.
e. I may have outgrown Halloween.
f. Three-day weekends make a lot of sense.

2. Afterward, reread your paragraph. It should have only one goal: developing the idea expressed in the topic sentence. Remove or alter any sentences that stray from that idea.

Remember

— *Effective paragraphs are unified.*
— *Every sentence in a unified paragraph works toward a single goal.*

LESSON **7**

Paragraph Development

You have probably noticed that in many paragraphs details support the statement made in a topic sentence. In Model 14, for example, a statement about the otter's restlessness when awake was supported by illustrative details of its overturning wastebaskets, throwing cushions on the floor, and the like. In the present lesson you will examine various kinds of details that may be used in developing paragraphs.

DEVELOPING WITH EXAMPLES Often a writer's topic sentence is a generalization that can best be supported by specific examples. In the following paragraph about regiments in the American Civil War, an initial topic sentence is developed with examples to illustrate what the statement means.

15 Bruce Catton in *This Hallowed Ground*

Some regiments took on especial characteristics. The New York 7th was a dandy outfit,* private soldiers wearing tailor-made gray uniforms as trim as so many West Pointers, with hired cooks to prepare the meals. The 33rd Illinois, organized largely through the efforts of Charles E. Hovey, principal of the State Normal University, who became its colonel, had many college students and teachers in its ranks and was known, inevitably, as the "Brains

* **dandy outfit:** an elegantly dressed regiment.

regiment." All sorts of tales were circulated about it; privates discharged from its rolls for mental incapacity, it was said, promptly won officers' commissions in less brilliant regiments. The 8th Wisconsin was famous as the "Eagle regiment," because its Company C came to camp with a live eagle as mascot. A T-shaped perch was devised, and the bird — known as "Old Abe" — was carried between regimental and national flags wherever the regiment went. Old Abe was even taken into battle later on; he liked artillery fire and would flap his wings and scream loudly, but grew depressed and nervous under musketry fire. The eagle survived the war and was taken back to Wisconsin and became an essential feature of innumerable postwar veterans' reunions.

The Writer's Craft

1. What generalization about Union regiments does the topic sentence express? The author goes on to develop the paragraph by citing specific examples to show what that general statement means. His first example concerns the New York 7th, an outfit of dandies. What characteristic was taken on by the 33rd Illinois? by the 8th Wisconsin?

2. Without the specific examples, would you have understood the author's topic sentence as well as you do now? Would you have been convinced by it?

The paragraph below provides another instance of a topic sentence that is developed and clarified by means of factual examples.

16 Edwin Way Teale in *North with the Spring*

The changes of spring extend into every cranny of the hemisphere. Ocean tides reach their peak. In inland ponds the surface water gradually changes place with the water at the bottom. Babies born in the spring are, on the average, taller and heavier than those born at other times of the year. In spring, growing children gain most rapidly in height. The increase is almost twice that of a similar period in fall. The very chemical composition of our blood alters slightly in spring; we sense the coming of the season in our lifestream.

The Writer's Craft

1. The topic sentence expresses the general idea that changes occurring in spring extend in every direction. To support his generalization, the author furnishes specific examples: springtime, he tells us, is when ocean tides reach their peak. Find within the paragraph at least three other factual examples that support the topic sentence.

2. Taken alone, is the first sentence in Model 16 entirely convincing? Do the author's factual examples help convince you of the truth of what his topic sentence asserts?

Now You Try It

Select one of the topic sentences listed below to develop in a brief paragraph — or choose a topic sentence of your own for that purpose. In composing the paragraph, support the topic sentence with several specific examples.

  a. Cars have changed drastically in the last fifty years.
  b. Many foreign foods have become part of the American diet.
  c. Junior high is different from elementary school.
  d. News travels fast today.
  e. Good (bad) luck can take many forms.
  f. Our world is full of strange sights.
  g. Today's average housewife has a staff of servants — electrical ones.

DEVELOPING WITH AN INCIDENT   Frequently the idea expressed in a topic sentence is best supported by a brief story, an anecdote or incident. To illustrate his topic sentence, the author of·the following paragraph tells an incident about a famous Polish actress.

17   Stanley Kahan in *Introduction to Acting*

It is obvious that the voice can be an important asset to any actor. One of the famous legends of the theater tells of the wonderful vocal expressiveness of the great Polish actress Helena Modjeska. Once at a dinner party, when asked to perform one of her famous scenes for the assembled guests, the actress complied by giving a very brief monologue. Many onlookers were moved to tears by the gripping effect of Modjeska's eloquence, despite the fact that she performed the "scene" in Polish! After she had finished she was asked which great and touching selection she had chosen to move her audience so deeply. It must have been with a sly wink that she confided that in fact she had recited the Polish alphabet. Such effectiveness was made possible not only by her sense of the dramatic but by a supple and expressive voice, delicately tuned to a great versatility and the needs of every occasion.

The Writer's Craft

1. The topic sentence states a generalization about an actor's voice. What is that general idea? Does the incident about Helena Modjeska support the topic sentence effectively? Explain.

2. Compare the model above with the following variation of it:

It is obvious that the voice can be an important asset to any actor. The great eighteenth-century actor David Garrick had a fine voice, and so did Henry Irving in the nineteenth century. In our own day, such famous actors as Sir Laurence Olivier and Sir John Gielgud, as well as actresses like Dame Edith Evans and Katharine Cornell, have performed their many memorable roles with voices that have been trained to express emotion in ways an ordinary, untrained voice simply is not capable of doing. Of course an actor's gestures and movements are important to his success, but his voice is extremely important too.

What is the difference between the way the two paragraphs develop the topic sentence? Which paragraph strikes you as more effective? Why?

Now You Try It

Select one of the topic sentences below — or a topic sentence of your own choosing — to develop in a brief paragraph. The topic sentence should be supported with an incident, either one you took part in, one someone told you about, or one you have read about.

a. The voice can be an important asset to a student.
b. Stage fright can be overpowering.
c. Safety belts are not merely decorations.
d. I no longer trust weather reports.
e. Accepting a dare can lead to surprising consequences.

DEVELOPING WITH REASONS Many topic sentences seem to invite the question "Why?" They may express an opinion like "I enjoy fishing," or they may make a direct claim like "Man needs the winds." In either case, alert readers finish the sentence wondering about it. A good way to develop such a topic sentence is to give reasons — details (either examples, incidents, or additional statements) that explain why the statement is true. Here is a paragraph that makes a direct claim, which it then supports with reasons.

Large industries are rarely located away from large water supplies. Not only is the water needed for transportation, but it is also usually needed in the manufacturing process. Many things have to be washed. Wastes have to be dumped out. Steam may be needed. Water may be necessary to dissolve materials. It may be used as a chemical in the manufacture of a material such as nylon, where it is combined with carbon from coal and gases from the air. For all of these reasons the factory is usually located where water is plentiful and cheap.

The Writer's Craft

1. The author begins his paragraph with the claim that big industries are rarely located far from large water supplies. He then gives reasons that tell why his topic sentence is true. For one thing, water is needed for transportation as well as for manufacturing. Moreover, in the process of manufacturing, water is needed for washing and also for dumping wastes. Find at least two other reasons given in the paragraph to support the claim of the topic sentence.

2. Imagine that claim standing alone, without the support of reasons. Do the reasons given help make the topic sentence convincing? Would you be satisfied with the opening statement of the paragraph if it were unsupported?

Now You Try It

Use one of the following topic sentences, or one of your own choosing, in a brief paragraph that you develop with reasons. The reasons you give may be either examples or incidents, but be sure that each reason supports the opinion or claim that your topic sentence states.

a. School routine should (should not) be varied frequently.

b. The wild turkey, not the bald eagle, should be our national bird.
c. Snacks are bad for your health.
d. It should be summer all year round.
e. Speeders deserve jail sentences.

. . . .

Remember

— *Paragraphs are often developed with specific details that support the topic sentence.*
— *Examples, incidents, and reasons are kinds of details frequently used.*

Coherence in Paragraphs

When a paragraph is coherent, its sentences are logically connected. In other words, the relationship between all the parts of the paragraph is logical and clear.

Coherence doesn't simply happen. On the contrary, it takes planning, just as it takes planning to achieve anything complex, whether a football play or a dance routine. To write coherently, the author first considers specific details that support his topic sentence, so that he may decide into what order those details fall most naturally. Then, after arranging the details in that order, he finds words that will indicate clearly to the reader just how the details are related. Of course, the experienced writer (like the experienced dancer or football player) executes the process more easily and successfully than the learner or amateur; but ordinarily, both amateurs and professionals must consciously strive for coherence if it is to be achieved.

CHRONOLOGICAL ORDER Ordinarily, in an account explaining how something works or how to do something or how something was done, the steps in the process fall naturally into chronological order. That is, they are most clearly presented in the order of their occurrence. Notice the arrangement of details in the following paragraph, which explains the final steps in the process by which Thomas Edison invented the electric light in 1878.

19 Floyd L. Darrow
in *Masters of Science and Invention*

He sent out immediately for a reel of cotton thread, and cutting off a suitable length, bent it horseshoe shape, clamped it in a nickel mold, and placed the mold in a muffle furnace. After five hours, he removed the mold, allowed it to 5 cool, and took out the precious filament. But it instantly broke. This process was repeated many times. Not until the evening of the third day was a filament successfully mounted, the air exhausted, and the current turned on. The light 10 that greeted the gaze of the experimenters seemed the most beautiful they had ever seen. Oblivious of their seventy-two hours without sleep, Edison and his assistant, Charles Bachelor, sat there and watched that first incandescent 15 lamp for forty hours more.

The Writer's Craft

1. Does the author make clear the steps that Edison took in solving the problem of providing a workable filament in an electric light? Would an explanation like the one given here be clear if the steps had not been presented in chronological order? Give reasons for your answer.

2. *Transitional expressions* are words and phrases that indicate how details are related to one another. In a paragraph with details arranged in chronological order, transitional expressions make it clear just when each step takes place. Some of these expressions are *before, first, next, afterward, then,*

the second step, at once, meanwhile, later, and *last of all.* In Model 19, the expression *after five hours* (lines 4–5) is transitional, here indicating how much time elapsed before the mold was removed. *Not until the evening of the third day* (line 8) is another such expression. What adverb in the opening sentence relates the time sequence of the paragraph to whatever may have gone before? What concluding phrase tells you how long Edison and his assistant watched the first incandescent lamp?

Now You Try It

In a short paragraph, explain how to do something with which you are familiar. If you wish you may explain how to do one of the following:

a. Assemble a machine or engine
b. Cut the grass
c. Remove a splinter
d. Drive a car
e. Study for a test
f. Pitch a curve
g. Bake a cake

In planning and writing your paragraph be sure to present details, or steps, in their natural chronological order. Use transitional expressions such as *first, afterward,* and *finally* to indicate clearly the order of the steps.

ORDER OF IMPORTANCE As you know, a topic sentence may make a general statement that the rest of the paragraph develops and supports with specific details. In such cases, one detail is often more important, or more significant, than the others. A good way to organize details that vary in importance is to arrange them so that the most important detail is either first or last. As an instance, notice the organization of the following paragraph.

20 John L. Chapman
in *Atlas: The Story of a Missile*

The countdown is partly a means of ensuring launchworthiness and partly a step-by-step process of giving the huge cylinder the ingredients it needs to achieve flight. Cool air is fed into areas containing hot electronics equipment. Helium, a light, colorless gas used to aid propellant flow and to actuate valves, is delivered to spherical storage bottles in the engine compartment. To increase the density of this gas (enabling more of it to be carried in a given space), liquid nitrogen, at a thermometer-shattering 320 degrees below zero (Fahrenheit), is pumped into shrouds around the helium bottles. Power for electrical systems, lubricating oil for pumps, and fluid for hydraulic lines are transferred to the missile. Most important of all, the propellants — more than a quarter million pounds of them — are pumped into the missile tanks.

The Writer's Craft

1. The topic sentence, which states that the countdown allows the missile to receive ingredients it needs for flight, is supported throughout the rest of the paragraph by mention of specific ingredients that the missile receives. What ingredients are mentioned? Of all those listed, which one does the author regard as the most important? How do you know?

2. Is the most important ingredient presented first or last? Is the arrangement used here an effective one for this paragraph? Explain your answer.

Now You Try It

Write a paragraph developing one of the topic sentences below or a topic sentence of your own choosing. Before beginning your composition, list the details that support your topic sentence. If one is more important than the others, save it for last, and either by means of adjectives (*the outstanding, the most impressive,* etc.) or transitional expressions (*above all, most important*) make sure your reader knows that it is the most important detail.

a. Driving is getting to be hazardous anywhere and anytime.
b. _____ is my favorite sport.
c. Men make the best cooks.
d. August is the worst (best) month.
e. Every family needs a pet.
f. Parades are boring.
g. Summer jobs have their advantages.

ORDER OF LOCATION   A descriptive paragraph will probably contain a number of details. One logical way to arrange those details is simply to follow them as they would appear in space. In other words, each detail in the paragraph can be presented on the basis of its location in the scene being described.

In the next paragraph, notice not only the order in which Gerald Durrell presents his details but also the way he makes their location clear.

21   Gerald Durrell in *The Overloaded Ark*

As you enter the forest, your eyes used to the glare of the sun, it seems dark and shadowy, and as cool as a butter dish. The light is filtered through a million leaves, and so has a curious green aquarium-like quality which makes every- 5 thing seem unreal. The centuries of dead leaves that have fluttered to the ground have provided a rich layer of mold, soft as any carpet, and giving off a pleasant earthy smell. On every side are the huge trees with their great curling buttress 10 roots, their thick smooth trunks towering hundreds of feet above, their head foliage and branches merging indistinguishably into the endless green roof of the forest. Between these the floor of the forest is covered with the young [15] trees, thin tender growths just shaken free of the cradle of leaf mold, long thin stalks with a handful of pale green leaves on top. They stand in the everlasting shade of their parents, ready for the great effort of shooting up to the life-giving sun. [20] In between their thin trunks, rambling across the floor of the forest, can be seen faint paths twisting and turning. These are the roads of the bush and are followed by all its inhabitants.

The Writer's Craft

1. The first sentence designates the scene to be described: the forest. The rest of the paragraph presents details of the scene. The author begins by describing the light in the forest (lines 3–6). Next he describes the floor of the forest (lines 6–9). Then he pictures the trees themselves: first the huge old trees (lines 9–14), then the thin young trees (lines 14–20). Finally Durrell describes the twisting paths between the trees (lines 21–24). Would you say that the whole paragraph is well organized?

2. The author follows the details in space, showing the location of one in relation to another. Does this organization help make his description clear? Explain.

3. Transitional expressions locate details in a descriptive paragraph. Some of these expressions are *beside, between, next to, under, among, on the edge, behind,* and *overhead.* Model 21 uses several transitional expressions to indicate the location of details. For example, the author locates the huge old trees by means of the phrase *on every side* (line 9). *Between these* (line 14) locates the thin young trees. In lines 11–23, find two transitional expressions that locate the twisting paths.

In a brief paragraph, describe a scene that you think is especially beautiful or interesting or memorable. You might describe a particular street, campsite, farmhouse, room, park, desert, waterfall, or river. But don't include every detail in the scene. Instead, pick out four or five details you consider outstanding; then decide on an effective order in which to present them. For instance, you may want to begin with the most impressive detail and then mention details surrounding it. Or you may decide to present the details as they exist in the scene, moving from nearest to farthest, highest to lowest, left to right, or in the reverse of any of those orders.

When ready to write, begin by naming the scene you are going to describe. Then present your details. Remember to make it clear to your reader just where each detail in the scene is located. Use transitional expressions wherever necessary.

. . . .

Remember

- *Good organization is the first step in achieving coherence.*
- *Three logical ways to arrange details are in chronological order, order of importance, and order of location.*
- *Transitional expressions help show the relationship between details.*

Choosing Words

LESSON

Nouns

In your writing, use the most precise nouns you can. Don't settle for *worker* or *man who fixes the wiring* when you mean *electrician*. Don't write *place where you get medical treatment* if you mean *clinic*.

The following passage contains Clarence Day's description of his father's office as it looked about seventy years ago. Notice the nouns that are used to name some of the people and objects in the office.

22   Clarence Day in *Life with Father*

The office was busy in what seemed to me a mysterious way. The cashier, who never would let me go inside his cage, sat in there on a stool, with a cash drawer, a safe full of books, another safe for securities, and a tin box full of postage stamps which he doled out as needed. One or two bookkeepers were making beautifully written entries in enormous leather-bound ledgers. They had taken the stiff white detachable cuffs off their shirtsleeves and stacked them in a corner, and they had exchanged their regular jackets for black alpaca coats. Future bookkeepers or brokers who now were little office boys ran in and out. Western Union messengers rushed in with telegrams. In the front room there was a long table full of the printed reports issued by railroads about their earnings and traffic. Only twenty or thirty industrial stocks were traded in on the Exchange in those days, and Father's office ignored them. On or around the table were the *Commercial & Financial Chronicle*, the *Journal of Commerce*, a blackboard, a ticker, and four or five whiskery men. Two were arguing heatedly about Henry Ward Beecher, and the others were shaking their heads over some crazy proposal by the "Knights of Labor" to have an eight-hour day.

The Writer's Craft

1. No doubt the author of this passage would have been dissatisfied with writing, "One man sat in his part of the office on a seat." Instead, Day wrote that a *cashier* sat in his *cage* on a *stool. Cashier, cage,* and *stool* are more precise nouns than *man, part,* and *seat.* Find at least three other precise nouns in the model, and explain how they help create a clear picture of the office. (Hint: Substitute less precise nouns and notice what happens.)

2. Using precise nouns means finding exact names rather than settling for a more general term that covers an entire group or class. Reread the sixth sentence in the model. Then suppose that the sentence had been written:

> Boys rushed in with messages.

Why is the above sentence, even though briefer, less effective than the one Day wrote?

3. After reading Day's description, you would surely recognize this office if you were to enter it. What specific objects and activities would enable you to recognize it?

Now You Try It

Write a brief description — perhaps a hundred words or so — of a place with which you are familiar. You might describe where your father works, or a dentist's waiting room, or your school auditorium during an assembly, or your family's kitchen, or any other place that you can recall vividly. Name specific persons and objects in the place, and use the most precise nouns you can think of to give your reader a clear, detailed picture.

The following selection considers some of the equipment used in underwater exploring. While reading it, watch for precise nouns.

23   Marston Bates in *The Forest and the Sea*

Man's eyes are of little use underwater, and fish watching depends on keeping the eyes in a pocket of air enclosed by some transparent material — goggles, masks, or helmets. It is curious how long it took Western man to realize this. [5] Helmets have been around for some time, but the complications of helmet diving gear restricted its use to professionals. The Japanese have long known the advantages of glass goggles, and the Polynesians saw the possibili- [10] ties when they realized there was such a thing as glass. But only in the 1930's did this idea spread from the Pacific to North America and Europe. The addition of an air tube, or snorkel, to the mask is even more recent. Many of us, as [15] children, must have played around with the idea of using a rubber breathing tube to stay underwater, but no one turned this into a practical apparatus until recently. Now, at any seaside resort, masks and snorkels are everywhere, and [20]

everywhere you see a few free spirits heading
out to sea with that remarkable invention of
Cousteau's, the aqualung, or with some modi-
fication of his basic idea. Flippers came along
incidentally, because only when you could see [25]
did it become important to have the hands free
— for spearing, for photographing, or for taking
notes on a plastic slate.

The Writer's Craft

1. To discuss a specialized activity like underwater exploring, a writer must know the various technical terms associated with it. Line 4 of the model contains three such
terms: *goggles, masks,* and *helmets.* Why do you suppose the author uses those precise nouns in addition to the
more general term that includes all three? In the model, find
another precise noun that names underwater equipment.

2. Ordinarily a precise noun like *goggles* is more effective than a roundabout expression like *spectacles designed to
protect the eyes.* But when a writer introduces a technical
term that may be unfamiliar to his readers, he will usually
take time to explain what it means. In lines 15–18, how does
Bates explain the meaning of *snorkel?* Is his explanation
clear?

The next model describes the huge fleet of ships
used by the Allies in the Normandy Invasion of World
War II. By means of precise nouns the author distin-
guishes among the many different ships that took part
in that invasion.

24   Cornelius Ryan
in *June 6, 1944: The Longest Day*

Now back in the Channel, plowing through
the choppy gray waters, a phalanx of ships bore
down on Hitler's Europe — the might and fury

of the free world unleashed at last. They came,
rank after relentless rank, ten lanes wide, twenty ⁵
miles across, five thousand ships of every description. There were fast new attack transports,
slow rust-scarred freighters, small ocean liners,
channel steamers, hospital ships, weather-beaten
tankers, coasters, and swarms of fussing tugs. ¹⁰
There were endless columns of shallow-draft
landing ships — great wallowing vessels, some of
them almost 350 feet long. Many of these and
the other heavier transports carried smaller landing craft for the actual beach assault — more ¹⁵
than 1,500 of them. Ahead of the convoys were
processions of minesweepers, coast guard cut-
ters, buoy layers, and motor launches. Barrage
balloons flew above the ships. Squadrons of
fighter planes weaved below the clouds. And ²⁰
surrounding this fantastic cavalcade of ships
packed with men, guns, tanks, motor vehicles,
and supplies, and excluding small naval vessels,
was a formidable array of 702 warships.

The Writer's Craft

1. Notice first that the author names more than a dozen
kinds of ships. Giving the exact names of so many ships increases the effectiveness of his description. How? Are there
any imprecise nouns in Model 24?

2. Besides names of ships, many other precise nouns appear in the model. In lines 19–20, for instance, Ryan writes,
"Squadrons of fighter planes weaved below the clouds." Why
is the precise noun *squadrons* better than *groups* or *numbers*
or *loads?* Find another precise noun in the model and explain
why it is a good choice. What additional explanation does
the author give for the precise term "shallow-draft landing
ships" (lines 11–12)?

Now You Try It

Choose one of the following:

1. Write a composition between 100 and 150 words long about a popular activity that makes use of its own distinctive vocabulary. Carpentry, boating, photography, baseball, bowling, and sewing are a few examples of many such activities. Briefly explain the activity and mention any recent developments in the equipment used. Remember to name objects exactly and to explain whatever technical terms your reader might not understand.

2. Write a brief description of some large-scale scene or event — for example, a crowd scene at a football game, circus, rodeo, or class picnic. Alternatively, you might describe an historical event as you picture it — a battle, a surrender, the signing of a treaty, a duel. In either case, use precise nouns to name the persons and objects in the scene.

....

Remember

— *Your writing should be exact.*
— *A precise noun provides the most effective way of naming a thing exactly.*

LESSON **10**
Adjectives

In the preceding lesson you learned the importance of choosing nouns with exact meanings. Sometimes, though, you cannot find a noun precise enough to express just the idea or picture you want to convey. At such times you may be able to write more precisely by using an adjective with a noun. But just as you must choose nouns carefully, you should be careful in choosing adjectives, those words that modify nouns. One well-chosen adjective is more effective than two or three hastily chosen ones. A *shrill* voice, for example, is more easily heard by your reader than a voice that you describe as *high* and *excited* and *angry*. A *luscious* plum is more exact and concise than one that you describe as *sweet, plump,* and *juicy.*

Many young writers make the mistake of using too many adjectives — usually because they do not take enough time to choose the best of the several that come to mind. If you do take time to choose thoughtfully, your writing will become more vivid.

The following paragraph describes Jo, a character in Louisa May Alcott's novel *Little Women.* Notice the adjectives used in the description.

25   Louisa May Alcott in *Little Women*

Fifteen-year-old Jo was tall, thin, and brown, and reminded one of a colt; for she never seemed to know what to do with her long limbs, which were very much in her way. She had a decided mouth, a comical nose, and sharp, gray eyes, ⁵ which appeared to see everything, and were by turns fierce, funny, or thoughtful. Her long, thick hair was her one beauty; but it was usually bundled into a net to be out of her way. Round shoulders had Jo, big hands and feet, a flyaway ¹⁰ look to her clothes, and the uncomfortable appearance of a girl who was rapidly shooting up into a woman, and didn't like it.

The Writer's Craft

1. The author has given a detailed picture of Jo, describing her appearance, her movements, even her personality. Carefully chosen adjectives are important in this kind of description. Find the adjective or adjectives that describe each of the following:

Jo's mouth (line 4)
her nose (line 5)
her eyes (lines 5–7)
her hair (lines 7–8)
her shoulders (lines 9–10)
her hands and feet (line 10)
the look of her clothes (lines 10–11)

Which of these adjectives do you find particularly effective? Why?

2. Louisa May Alcott does not use adjectives at every opportunity; she uses them only when she thinks they are effective. For example, she does not use an adjective in mentioning that Jo "reminded one of a colt." Why would it be less effective to write that Jo reminded one of an *awkward, gangly* colt?

Now You Try It

1. Write a brief description of someone you know well. Choosing adjectives carefully, describe the person's appearance in detail. But go further: try to give your reader an idea of what the person is like.

2. Afterward, reread your description. Be sure that all the adjectives are accurate and vivid. Most important, test what you have written by omitting each adjective and then deciding if the adjective is necessary and effective.

Now read this selection, which describes dusk on a farm in England.

26   John Galsworthy in "The Apple Tree"

Dusk had gathered thick. The farm buildings and the wheelhouse were all dim and bluish, the apple trees but a blurred wilderness; the air smelled of woodsmoke from the kitchen fire. One bird going to bed later than the others was uttering a halfhearted twitter, as though surprised at the darkness. From the stable came the snuffle and stamp of a feeding horse. And away over there was the loom * of the moor, and away and away the shy stars that had not as yet full light, pricking white through the deep blue heavens.

* **loom:** misty appearance.

The Writer's Craft

1. John Galsworthy did not describe the scene in the passage above merely because he enjoyed painting a word picture. Rather, he described it to create an overall effect. In his first two sentences, he uses the adjectives *thick, dim, bluish,* and *blurred.* What atmosphere do those adjectives help create? Is it an atmosphere suitable to the scene?

2. Look through the rest of the passage. Do you think Galsworthy chose his adjectives carefully, with a view toward the overall effect they would create? Explain.

Now You Try It

Write a brief description of a scene that creates a strong overall effect, or atmosphere. To create that atmosphere, choose your adjectives carefully. For example, in describing a mysterious house, you might find adjectives like *shadowy, deserted,* and *eerie* appropriate in helping to establish the air of mystery. Other scenes you might describe are the bustling activity of an intersection at rush hour, the serenity of a river on a summer afternoon, the tenseness of a classroom during a test, the sparkling beauty of a lake in the mountains. In selecting your adjectives, don't forget that one well-chosen adjective is more effective than several hastily chosen ones.

. . . .

Remember

- *A few well-chosen adjectives help make descriptions vivid and accurate.*
- *Use adjectives sparingly.*

Verbs

Suppose you are describing the final moments of the 100-yard dash at a track meet. You could write that the runners *moved* or *ran* toward the tape, but neither of those verbs forcefully conveys the speed and strain involved in such a race. By searching your mind for a minute, however, you will discover other, more precise verbs that might apply. *Dashed, sprinted,* and *streaked,* for instance, are all improvements over the more general verbs *moved* and *ran.*

Don't be satisfied with the first verb that occurs to you. As with nouns and adjectives, choose carefully. Take time to consider several verbs before selecting the one that most precisely conveys your meaning.

As you read the following selection, about a man's encounter with a panther, notice the verbs chosen to describe the action.

27 **Constance Rourke in *Davy Crockett***

In this forest, panthers lurked, robbing the hunter of the deer he had killed if he was not watchful, attacking men if startled close at hand. A settler in this region was walking up and down in his cabin with a child in his arms one evening. The door was open, and as he turned away from it a panther slipped in. The door was slammed

5

shut by a sudden wind, the man turned quickly,
the panther crouched and sprang. The settler
dropped the child and slid to the floor so as to [10]
get the beast under him, and by a sudden
wrench succeeded in turning so that he could
seize the panther by the throat. The strong grasp
loosened the animal's hold, and with a ferocious
strength the settler rose and hurled him into the [15]
wide fireplace where a great pile of hickory logs
was burning. Choked and blinded by smoke,
singed by the fire, the panther ran up the chim-
ney, out on the roof, leapt, and fled.

The Writer's Craft

1. By trying to supply a substitute for *lurked* in line 1,
you will discover how sound the writer's judgment was in
choosing that verb. Substitute *hid* or *remained*. Are either of
those verbs as good as *lurked* to suggest the panthers' watchful waiting?

2. In this passage the violent action is vivid and exciting,
mainly because of the author's well-chosen verbs. *Crouched*
and *sprang* (line 9), for instance, describe the movements of
a panther about as vividly as words can. Find at least three
other verbs in the model that strike you as particularly vivid.

Now You Try It

Describe a scene filled with action — a fight, an automo-
bile accident, a successful football play, an exciting hunting
or fishing experience, a chase. Choose verbs that make the
actions clear and vivid. When several verbs occur to you, select the one that describes the action most effectively.

> On first thought you might not suppose that a recipe
> requires carefully chosen verbs. Yet the following se-
> lection from a cookbook shows that even in a recipe,
> verbs play a key part in effective writing.

Put the rice and all the seasonings except the onion into the boiling water; then cover and simmer it fifty minutes. Stir it occasionally, and add a little more water if you need to. While this is going on, sauté the onion in half the butter until ⁵ it is very light brown; then add the chicken livers and cook five minutes. Now mix the chicken livers, onion, and rice together; pour it into a buttered casserole; and dot it with the rest of the butter. Sprinkle a little Parmesan on top and ¹⁰ bake it, uncovered, at 375° for fifteen minutes.

The Writer's Craft

1. Some verbs in this selection — *put, cover, add* — are unexceptional; nevertheless, they are effective because they are the right verbs for the author's purpose. Other verbs, not so ordinary, were carefully chosen for their precise meanings. Precision is especially important in giving directions. What, for example, is the meaning of *simmer* (lines 2–3)? of *sauté* (line 5)? of *bake* (line 11)? Can you think of an adequate substitute for any of those precise verbs? In the model, find two other verbs with equally precise meanings.

2. The quality of the verbs you use depends on the number you can call to mind to describe an action. In other words, the more verbs you are able to choose from, the better your final choice will be. In this passage the verbs *simmer, sauté,* and *bake* are precise verbs used in place of the more general verb *cook*. List as many other substitutes for *cook* as you can think of. Explain the meaning of each word in your list.

Now You Try It

Choose a task that requires a variety of actions; then write a brief explanation of how the task should be performed. You might write about preparing a dinner, putting up a hammock, delivering newspapers, knitting a sweater, or coaching a team from the sidelines. To make your explanation clear, select the most precise verb you can think of for each action you describe.

> From the great open spaces of the desert, the writer of the following model watched a flight of migrating birds approaching and passing overhead. Notice the exactness of the verbs used to describe their flight.

29 Loren Eiseley in *The Immense Journey*

I saw the flight coming on. It was moving like a little close-knit body of black specks that danced and darted and closed again. It was pouring from the north and heading toward me with the undeviating relentlessness of a compass needle. It streamed through the shadows rising out of monstrous gorges. It rushed over towering pinnacles in the red light of the sun, or momentarily sank from sight within their shade. Across that desert of eroding clay and wind-worn stone they came with a faint wild twittering that filled all the air about me as those tiny living bullets hurtled past into the night.

The Writer's Craft

1. Verbs, like adjectives, can help create the overall effect of a particular scene. In the passage above, the author creates an effect of continuous movement, which contrasts with the stillness of the desert. Find at least three well-chosen verbs used to describe the continuous movement of the birds.

2. It is interesting to note that the verb *fly* does not appear anywhere in the description. Surely when a writer is describing a flock of migrating birds, *fly* must be one of the

first words that occur to him. Why do you think Eiseley decided against using that word? To test his decision, see if any verb in the model is less effective than *fly*.

Now You Try It

Write a brief description of a scene in which a good deal of action takes place, making use of precise verbs that describe the action vividly. Your subject might be the corridors of your school between classes, the last game of a championship athletic contest, a crowded swimming pool in August, an anthill, or a sale in a department store. If the scene you choose evokes a single overall effect, select verbs that help create that effect in your description.

. . . .

Remember

— *Carefully chosen verbs help describe action vividly.*
— *In telling how to do something, use verbs with precise meanings.*

LESSON **12**

Adverbs

Used with a verb, an adverb indicates how, when, or where the action of the verb occurs. Used with another adverb or with an adjective, an adverb gives a somewhat different shade of meaning to the word it modifies.

For example, the sentence, "The stranger began to speak in a low voice" may leave some relevant questions unanswered. If the writer wants to convey additional information, he may add adverbs: "*Then* the stranger began to speak in a *menacingly* low voice." The adverb *then* tells when the stranger spoke; the adverb *menacingly* gives additional meaning to *low*, an adjective.

The next selection, from a story by Jack London, is about a prospector in gold-rush days. Consider especially the author's use of adverbs to describe the prospector's movements as he pans for gold.

30   **Jack London in "All-Gold Canyon"**

He crossed the stream below the pool, stepping agilely from stone to stone. Where the side-hill touched the water, he dug up a shovelful of dirt and put it into the gold pan. He squatted down, holding the pan in his two hands, and ⁵ partly immersing it in the stream. Then he imparted to the pan a deft circular motion that sent the water sluicing * in and out through the dirt and gravel. The larger and the lighter particles worked to the surface, and these, by a skillful [10] dipping movement of the pan, he spilled out and over the edge. Occasionally, to expedite ° matters, he rested the pan and with his fingers raked out the large pebbles and pieces of rock.

The contents of the pan diminished rapidly [15] until only fine dirt and the smallest bits of gravel remained. At this stage he began to work very deliberately and carefully. It was fine washing, and he washed fine and finer, with a keen scrutiny and delicate and fastidious touch. At last [20] the pan seemed empty of everything but water; but with a quick semicircular flirt † that sent the water flying over the shallow rim into the stream, he disclosed a layer of black sand on the bottom of the pan. So thin was this layer that it was like [25] a streak of paint. He examined it closely. In the midst of it was a tiny golden speck. He dribbled a little water in over the depressed edge of the pan. With a quick flirt he sent the water sluicing across the bottom, turning the grains of black [30] sand over and over. A second tiny golden speck rewarded his effort.

The washing had now become very fine — fine beyond all need of ordinary placer mining.‡ He worked the black sand, a small portion at a time, [35] up the shallow rim of the pan. Each small portion he examined sharply, so that his eyes saw every grain of it before he allowed it to slide over the

---

* **sluicing:** flowing.
° **expedite:** speed up.
† **flirt:** a quick toss or flick.
‡ **placer mining:** searching for valuable deposits by washing the soil.

edge and away. Jealously, bit by bit, he let the
black sand slip away. A golden speck, no larger ⁴⁰
than a pinpoint, appeared on the rim, and by his
manipulation of the water it returned to the bottom of the pan. And in such fashion another
speck was disclosed, and another. Great was his
care of them. Like a shepherd he herded his ⁴⁵
flock of golden specks so that not one should be
lost. At last, of the pan of dirt nothing remained
but his golden herd. He counted it, and then,
after all his labor, set it flying out of the pan with
one final swirl of water. 50

The Writer's Craft

1. This passage describes a complicated operation, but
in a way that keeps the reader from becoming confused.
Partly through well-chosen adverbs, London manages not
only to include dozens of different actions but also to make
each one distinct and clear. Look back at some of the adverbs
in the model and at the words they modify. The adverb
agilely (line 2) modifies *stepping*, a verb form called a "par-
ticiple." The adverb *down* (line 5) modifies *squatted*, a verb.
Find five other adverbs in the passage and tell what words
they modify.

2. Notice that the adverbs in this model suggest certain
things about the prospector. Lines 17–18, for example, tell
us that the prospector began to work *deliberately* and *carefully*. Other adverbs describing his movements are *closely*
(line 26), *sharply* (line 37), and *jealously* (line 39). From
those adverbs alone, what can you guess about the prospector's feelings as he works?

The following selection relates the experience of a
man trying to climb down a rocky precipice high above
a fast-moving stream. When the large roots that have

been supporting him suddenly begin to tear loose, he nearly plunges into the torrent below. As you read, notice the adverbs that help make the experience vivid.

31   Herman Melville in *Typee*

As one after another the treacherous roots yielded to my grasp, and fell into the torrent, my heart sank within me. The branches on which I was suspended over the yawning chasm swung to and fro in the air, and I expected them every ⁵ moment to snap in twain.* Appalled at the dreadful fate that menaced me, I clutched frantically at the only large root which remained near me, but in vain; I could not reach it, though my fingers were within a few inches of it. Again ¹⁰ and again I tried to reach it, until at length, maddened with the thought of my situation, I swayed myself violently by striking my foot against the side of the rock, and at the instant that I approached the large root, caught desperately at it, ¹⁵ and transferred myself to it. It vibrated violently under the sudden weight, but fortunately did not give way.

* **in twain:** in two.

The Writer's Craft

1. Adverbs can indicate how, when, or where an action happens. In this model the most effective adverbs let the reader know exactly how certain actions occurred. *Violently* (line 16) is such an adverb; it tells how the large root vibrated. Find three adverbs in the model that tell how the man performed actions.

2. Can you suggest why a writer describing an experience like this one might be chiefly concerned with indicating *how* different actions occur?

Now You Try It

Choose one of the following:

1. Write a brief description of someone engaged in a complicated operation which, like panning for gold, requires considerable skill. Some suggestions: a house painter painting a wall, a barber giving a crew cut, a quarterback executing a forward pass, a workman mixing and pouring cement. To describe each movement, select your verbs carefully, and use adverbs only where they are needed to sharpen your description of certain actions. If possible, choose adverbs that suggest the feelings of the person performing the operation.

2. Briefly describe an experience, real or imagined, in which you faced grave danger. Select adverbs that will impress your reader with the vast problems that confronted you and the efforts required to overcome them. In describing your actions, use verbs that indicate exactly how they were carried out. When necessary, modify the verbs with adverbs to give just the right shade of meaning. Try also to use adverbs that suggest your feelings during the experience.

> If you have ever picked up a sled, run hard with it to give yourself a good start, then dropped down on it for a fast ride, you will appreciate the accuracy of the description in this model.

32   Thomas E. Adams in "Sled"

Then he started to trot slowly down the street. Slowly, slowly gaining speed without losing balance. Faster he went now, watching the snow glide beneath his shiny black rubbers. Faster and faster, but stiffly, don't slip. Don't fall, don't ⁵ fall: now! And his body plunged downward, and the sled whacked in the quiet, and the white close to his eyes was flying beneath him as he felt the thrill of gliding alone along a shadowy street, with only the ski sound of the sled in the ¹⁰ packed snow. Then before his eyes the moving snow gradually slowed. And stopped. And he heard only the low sound of the wind and his breath.

Up again and start the trot. He moved to the [15] beating sound of his feet along the ground. His breath came heavily and quickly, and matched the rhythm of his pumping legs, straining to carry the weight of his body without the balance of his arms. He reached a wild dangerous [20] breakneck speed, and his leg muscles swelled and ached from the tension, and the fear of falling too early filled his mind; and down he let his body go. The white road rushed to meet him; he was off again, guiding the sled obliquely across [25] the street toward a huge pile of snow near a driveway.

The Writer's Craft

1. What is the effect of repeating the adverbs *slowly* and *faster* at the beginning of the model? The adverbs *stiffly* (line 5) and *heavily* and *quickly* (line 17) help convey an impression of the boy's feelings. Describe that impression.

2. This selection makes good use of adverbs that indicate when actions occurred. *Then*, in lines 1 and 11, is such an adverb. What adverb in line 6 lets the reader know when something happened?

3. Adverbs should be used only where they are necessary. In line 7, the author writes that "the sled whacked in the quiet." Why is no adverb necessary there? Suppose, having been unable to think of the verb *whacked*, the author had written that "the sled hit noisily in the quiet." Why is *whacked*, a precise verb, more effective than *hit noisily*, a more general verb modified by an adverb? In lines 9–10, Adams mentions "a shadowy street." Why is a well-chosen adjective like *shadowy* more effective than an adverb-adjective combination like *poorly lighted?*

Now You Try It

Write a brief description of someone doing something you yourself have often done. You might write about someone diving from a low board, throwing snowballs, climbing a tree, tossing a ball off a wall, or jumping rope. Choose your adverbs to describe the person's actions precisely and, if possible, to suggest his feelings. Be sure, though, that you use adverbs only where necessary. Remember that they cannot do the work of precise verbs or of well-chosen descriptive adjectives. For example, if the adjective *chilly* does not really convey your meaning, don't simply add an adverb and write *extremely chilly*. Try instead to think of a more accurate adjective, like *icy,* to convey your meaning.

. . . .

Remember

— *Adverbs help describe action sharply and clearly.*

— *Adverbs can suggest a person's feelings as he acts.*

— *Properly used, adverbs strengthen your writing; but don't overuse them.*

Description

LESSON **13**

Using Specific Details

Anyone learning to write should practice description; it is important in almost every kind of composition. Whether he is composing a story, an explanation, or an essay of opinion, the writer will frequently find himself describing persons, places, or objects in order to convey his meaning effectively.

A description is made up of details. But because mentioning every detail about a subject would only confuse the reader, the writer of a description must decide which details to include and which to omit. On what basis does he decide? He selects those details that best help to achieve his purpose in writing the description. If, for instance, he is writing about a family living in poverty on a run-down farm, he will no doubt describe the farm by selecting only those details that show how unproductive and impoverished it is.

In a clear description details are as specific as the writer can make them. The following model contains a description of a Chinese tracker — a man who travels on board a ship under sail and goes ashore to tow whenever necessary. As you read, watch for specific details of the man's appearance.

33   John Hersey in *A Single Pebble*

As the lugsail was taken in and the junk was rowed toward the left bank by a squad of trackers, I noticed that one of them, a lumpy, broad-

faced fellow with a shaven head, who was
dressed in new blue cotton pants and a drab ⁵
ragged jacket, took the lead in all that was done.
From his powerful larynx to his square feet, this
man, whom the owner addressed with a nickname, Old Pebble, seemed to be one whole,
rhythm-bound muscle. Everything he did had ¹⁰
rhythm. As he gave orders on board the junk, he
kicked his feet on the slapping unbolted planks
of the deck; he punctuated what he said with
tongue clicks; his hands moved in rope-pulling
gestures, all in time with his cadenced speech. ¹⁵
His head was spherical, and he had the crow's
feet of cheerfulness all the way from his narrow
eyes back to his ears. I have never been able to
tell with certainty how old a Chinese is; I would
guess that this one was in his mid-thirties. At ²⁰
any rate, the "Old" of his nickname was surely an
affectionate term; he seemed young and strong.
I saw that he wore a silver ring, and although
his hands had no more grace than monkey
wrenches, he had let his fingernails grow rather ²⁵
long, in the old style, evidently to show that he
was of the boatmen's nobility.

The Writer's Craft

1. This description contains details carefully chosen to
give a clear picture of Old Pebble. In addition to describing
the man's face, head, pants, jacket, and feet, the author mentions various other details of his appearance. Find at least
three other details about Old Pebble in the model.

2. A good description is more than merely a list of details.
The details must be specific. To make them so, a writer provides additional information about them. One of the details
here, for example, is Old Pebble's head, which Hersey tells
us was "shaven" (line 4) and "spherical" (line 16). Find

additional information that makes each of the following details specific:

Old Pebble's pants (lines 4–5)
his jacket (lines 5–6)
his feet (line 7)
the movement of his hands (lines 14–15)
his eyes (lines 17–18)
his ring (line 23)

Notice specific details that the author of the following model has included to describe a typical colonial town in Mexico.

34   John A. Crow in *Mexico Today*

The streets are long treeless lanes paved with cobblestones, bordered by narrow sidewalks, both deliberately made narrow in order to give some refuge from the tropical sun. The houses stand one next to the other in continuous and ⁵ unbroken lines, and are flush with the sidewalk, as if a yard or garden either between or in front of them were an impossible conception. Ordinarily the houses are of a single story, but in some of the larger centers they will have two ¹⁰ stories, with balconies and iron-barred windows on the second floor overlooking the street. First-floor windows are also invariably protected by iron grilles, backed up by solid wood blinds which swing inward to open. Sometimes, too, ¹⁵ there is a wrought-iron railing over the entrance. Externally, the colonial houses have a massive, severe appearance. The façades are seldom decorated, except for the enormous wooden doors which are of beams so huge that it would take a ²⁰ battering ram to knock them down.

The Writer's Craft

1. The author of this description mentions many details. To make them specific, he gives additional information about them: the streets, he tells us, "are long treeless lanes paved with cobblestones"; the houses "stand one next to the other in continuous and unbroken lines." Find at least two other specific details in the description.

2. Precise nouns help make details specific. *Lanes* (line 1) is a more precise noun than *streets*. Explain how its use here changes your mental picture of the streets of the Mexican town. With what precise nouns does the author name the following?

the material used to pave the streets (line 2)
the iron gratings that protect the first-floor windows (line 14)
the front parts of the houses (line 18)
the heavy pieces of wood used in the doors (line 20)

3. Adjectives, too, are useful in making details specific. *Long* and *treeless* (line 1) help give a clear picture of the streets in the town. Find the adjectives that make the following details specific:

sidewalks (line 2)
windows (line 11)
doors (line 19)
beams (line 20)

Now read the following description of the Nebraska countryside in winter.

35   Willa Cather in *O Pioneers!*

Winter has settled down over the Divide again; the season in which Nature recuperates, in which she sinks to sleep between the fruitfulness of autumn and the passion of spring.

The birds have gone. The teeming life that goes ⁵
on down in the long grass is exterminated. The
prairie dog keeps his hole. The rabbits run
shivering from one frozen garden patch to another and are hard put to it to find frostbitten
cabbage stalks. At night the coyotes roam the ¹⁰
wintry waste, howling for food. The variegated
fields are all one color now; the pastures, the
stubble, the roads, the sky are the same leaden
gray. The hedgerows and trees are scarcely per-
ceptible against the bare earth, whose slaty hue ¹⁵
they have taken on. The ground is frozen so hard
that it bruises the foot to walk in the roads or in
the plowed fields. It is like an iron country, and
the spirit is oppressed by its rigor and melan-
choly.
                                                    ²⁰

The Writer's Craft

1. To appreciate the importance of specific details in this
selection, compare it with the following brief description that
omits most of those details:

> In Nebraska in winter there are no birds or insects,
> and the animals are cold and hungry. Everything looks
> gray. The ground is frozen.

Explain how the inclusion of specific details in the model
clarifies each of the bare statements above.

2. In her last sentence Willa Cather compares Nebraska
in winter to "an iron country." The comparison suggests her
purpose in writing the description. Explain how the following details help support the effect she is striving for:

the color of the fields, pastures, stubble, roads, and sky
(lines 11–14)
the color of the hedgerows and trees (lines 14–16)
the hardness of the ground (lines 16–18)

Does any detail in the model *not* support the "iron-country"
effect?

3. In description, selection is vital. Here, for example, the author has not included everything about Nebraska winters that may have occurred to her. Instead, she has selected only those details that help her achieve her purpose. Consider these two details:

the shouts and laughter of children tobogganing
the glitter and sparkle of snow under a winter sky

Would Willa Cather have mentioned either of those details, even if they had actually existed in the scene she was describing? Would they have helped her achieve an iron-country effect? Explain.

WORD CHOICE

Often the effect of a description is heightened by suggestion in place of direct statement. For example, Willa Cather avoids stating directly that the rabbits were cold. In fact, nowhere in the paragraph does she use the word *cold*. What she does use are details that skillfully *suggest* cold. Which words in the following sentence do so?

> The rabbits run shivering from one frozen garden patch to another and are hard put to it to find frostbitten cabbage stalks.

Now You Try It

In this lesson you have read three vivid descriptions — one of a man, one of a town, and one of a winter countryside. The following assignments are based on those models. In considering each assignment, remember that it is good practice to describe only persons, places, or things you have actually seen. Since most effective descriptions grow out of close observation, you should not at this time try to describe a scene entirely from your imagination.

Choose one of the following:

1. In 100–150 words, write a description of someone *you have observed closely*. The description will be easier to write

if you choose a person whose appearance is in some way interesting, unusual, or distinctive. First decide what overall impression of the person you want to create. Your purpose might be to show that he is particularly careless, energetic, studious, good-natured, vain, or absent-minded. With a purpose clearly in mind, jot down details about the person that will help you achieve it. Then write your description. Afterward, reread it. Have you selected details that together create a single overall impression? Omit any that do not. Have you chosen adjectives carefully and used precise nouns to make the details as specific as possible?

2. Write a brief description of an interesting street or neighborhood *with which you are familiar*. Your purpose in describing the place might be to show that it is luxurious, overcrowded, noisy, friendly, picturesque, or dull. Select details — buildings, people, cars, lampposts, trees, and bushes — that help you achieve your purpose. When you finish, reread the description, making sure that each detail is as specific as you can picture it in words. Revise where necessary.

3. Describe a landscape — a seacoast, lakefront, field, wooded area, mountain range — *that is familiar to you*. Portray the place at a particular time of year, and try to create a single strong impression, as Willa Cather created an iron-country effect in her description of Nebraska. Remember that the success of your description depends not only on the specific details you choose but also on how well they combine to create a single impression.

. . . .

Remember

— *Specific details are essential in a clear description.*
— *Include only those details that help you achieve your purpose in writing the description.*

LESSON **14**

Showing the Location of Details

The description of a place will gain in clarity if details composing it are located according to some logical plan. In describing a room, for example, a writer might move methodically about it, describing what is located on each side of the room in turn. Alternatively, he might begin with a general impression as he steps inside, then describe the first detail that attracts his attention — a colorful rug or an easy chair perhaps. He might then proceed to mention less prominent surrounding objects. In that case his plan would be to mention details as they caught his eye.

Either of those two approaches could be effective. There are other approaches as well, but whichever one is chosen, the writer must have some kind of plan, one that the reader will be able to follow. To clarify his plan and the location of the details, the writer will find that such transitional expressions as *to the left, in front of, behind,* and *above* are essential.

The next model describes a memorable ruin of a civilization long since vanished from the heights of the Andes in Peru. About A.D. 1000 the Tiahuanaco people abandoned their monumental city 13,000 feet above sea level for reasons still not understood. Through the centuries that followed, the structures they left behind, surrounding a deserted public square, or Calasasaya, mouldered unregarded. Visitors nowadays ascend the steep mountain and gaze in awe at those vast remnants of a mysterious race.

36   Robert Silverberg in *Empires in the Dust*

In one corner of the Calasasaya is the eeriest of all the Tiahuanaco ruins: a gateway, standing alone, leading nowhere. "The Gateway of the Sun," it is called. Carved from a ten-ton block of lava, it is ten feet high, twelve and a half feet ⁵ wide. A rectangular doorway cut in the center is surrounded by carvings in the strange Tiahuanaco style, and above the doorway is a large figure, facing front and holding a staff in each hand. From his head sprout condors and puma- ¹⁰ heads, which are repeated elsewhere on his body, and from his belt dangles a row of faces. Surrounding him are forty-eight attendants, running toward him in eternally frozen motion, shown in profile with the faces of condors. It is a terrify- ¹⁵ ing sight, this gateway to nowhere. The visitor, already numbed by the cold and dizzied by the thinness of the air, trembles with wonder as he beholds it.

The Writer's Craft

1. Where on the Calasasaya is the Gateway of the Sun located? What is in the center of the gateway? Where does the gateway lead?

2. The description is clear because the author is careful throughout to give the location of details he mentions. He writes, for example, that "*above* the doorway is a large figure"

(lines 8–9). Find the word or phrase that locates each of the following details:

the carvings on the gateway (lines 6–7)
the two staffs belonging to the figure (lines 9–10)
the "row of faces" (line 12)
the forty-eight attendants (lines 12–15)

3. Can you explain the author's plan in this description? Might it have been equally effective to start from the left of the gateway and move horizontally to the right, describing what would be seen in turn? Discuss.

WORD CHOICE

A description like this gains from the inclusion of words that help express the mystery and uniqueness of what is being pictured. *Eeriest* (line 1) is one such word; *strange* (line 7) is another. What other words help invest the gateway and its surroundings with a distinctive atmosphere?

In the following selection Herbert Read describes a farmhouse he remembers from his boyhood.

37   Herbert Read in *The Innocent Eye*

The farmhouse was a square stone box with a roof of vivid red tiles. Its front was to the south, and warm enough to shelter some apricot trees against the wall, but there was no traffic that way. All our exits and entrances were made on ⁵ the north side, through the kitchen; and I think even our grandest visitors did not disdain that approach. Why should they? On the left as they entered direct into the kitchen was an old oak dresser; on the right a large open fireplace, with ¹⁰ a great iron kettle hanging from the reckan,*

* **reckan:** large hook.

and an oven to the near side of it. A long deal *
table, glistening with a honey-gold sheen from
much scrubbing, filled the far side of the room;
long benches ran down each side of it. The floor ¹⁵
was flagged with stone, each stone neatly out-
lined with a border of Bath brick,° rubbed on
after each washing. Sides of bacon and plump
dusky hams hung from the beams of the wooden
ceiling. ²⁰

* **deal:** fir or pinewood.
° **Bath brick:** unfired brick used as a polish.

The Writer's Craft

1. The author of this passage planned his description
carefully. Why do you think he began with the exterior of the
farmhouse? If he had begun with the entrance to the kitchen,
had next described the house from the outside, and then described the kitchen itself, would you have been able to picture the place clearly? Explain.

2. The author follows a plan in describing the kitchen interior. What is it?

3. The location of nearly every detail is given in the passage. For example, we are told that the front of the farmhouse
was *to the south* (line 2), but that all the "exits and entrances were made *on the north side*" (lines 5–6). What
phrases locate each of the following:

the dresser (lines 8–9)
the fireplace (line 10)
the table (lines 12–14)

4. As in the preceding model, some details of Read's description are located in relation to others. Consider lines 2–4.
After explaining that the front wall of the farmhouse faced
south, the author states that the apricot trees were against
the wall. In line 10 he mentions the fireplace; then in line
12 he indicates that the oven was on the near side of the
fireplace. In relation to what object does he locate the
benches (line 15)?

The author uses many well-chosen adjectives to make his details specific. With what adjectives does he describe the following:

the roof tiles (line 2)
the dresser (line 9)
the fireplace (line 10)
the kettle (line 11)
the table (line 12)
the sheen of the table (lines 13–14)
the hams (lines 18–19)
the ceiling (line 19)

Choose two of Read's adjectives that you think particularly effective, and be prepared to account for your choices.

This model describes a room — the study of a very strange doctor who lived a long time ago. Notice how precisely each detail in the room is located.

**38   Nathaniel Hawthorne
in "Dr. Heidegger's Experiment"**

If all stories were true, Dr. Heidegger's study must have been a very curious place. It was a dim, old-fashioned chamber, festooned with cobwebs, and besprinkled with antique dust. Around the walls stood several oaken bookcases, ⁵ the lower shelves of which were filled with rows of gigantic folios and black-letter quartos, and the upper with little parchment-covered duodecimos. Over the central bookcase was a bronze bust of Hippocrates, with which, according to some au- ¹⁰ thorities, Dr. Heidegger was accustomed to hold consultations in all difficult cases of his practice.

In the obscurest corner of the room stood a tall and narrow oaken closet, with its door ajar, within which doubtfully appeared a skeleton. [15] Between two of the bookcases hung a looking glass, presenting its high and dusty plate within a tarnished gilt frame. Among many wonderful stories related of this mirror, it was fabled that the spirits of all the doctor's deceased patients [20] dwelt within its verge,* and would stare him in the face whenever he looked thitherward.

* **verge:** boundaries.

The Writer's Craft

1. Set down the expressions used to locate each of the following:

the oaken bookcases (line 5)
the bust of Hippocrates (lines 9–10)
the oaken closet (lines 14–15)
the looking glass (line 16)

2. Notice Hawthorne's plan. He opens with a general statement: "If all stories were true, Dr. Heidegger's study must have been a very curious place." Why do you think the author began that way? He could have given the details first and used the general statement as a kind of summary or conclusion. Which arrangement for this paragraph do you consider more effective? Why?

Now You Try It

Everyone knows a few places that have made a lasting impression on him. Some are vividly remembered for their beauty or uniqueness. Others, of course, are remembered for their unpleasantness. Still others are recalled clearly because they are so familiar. Search your memory for a place you remember so well that it could serve as the subject of a detailed description. The following are general suggestions:

a. a city street
b. a public building
c. a playground
d. an unusual room
e. a bus
f. a church
g. a department store

In 100–150 words, write a description that will let readers see the place distinctly.

Bear in mind that the purpose of this assignment is to give you practice in locating details included in a description. Accordingly, use as many locating expressions as you find necessary. Of course, the success of your description will largely depend on how well you make and follow a plan, and what you write will also show how well you have mastered the skills of choosing specific details and using precise words. If you can invest your description with a distinctive atmosphere, so much the better.

. . . .

Remember

— *In describing a place, make and follow a plan.*
— *Clearly indicate the location of details in your description.*

LESSON **15**

Using Sensory Details

Good description grows out of a writer's experience, and experience comes through the senses — through seeing, hearing, touching, smelling, and tasting. Walking into school in the morning, you experience the school through your senses. You *see* the corridors, classmates at their lockers, teachers hurrying to their rooms — a confused scene full of movement and color. You *hear* the voices of those around you, the slamming of locker doors, the shrill ringing of the bell. You *feel* the different temperature inside the building, the other students crowding past, the contours of a classroom chair as you take your seat. Perhaps, too, you *smell* the familiar odors of chalk dust and cleaning compound. All of your senses are involved except the sense of taste. (That, too, may be involved if you are nervous about an approaching test and find your mouth unnaturally dry.) In fact, there is not a moment during your waking hours when your senses are not helping you experience your surroundings.

If you want to describe a certain experience vividly, include *sensory details,* all those details that appeal to the senses. And the details you include should appeal to as many different senses as appropriate. Here, as an illustration, is a description of an autumn afternoon. Notice to how many senses it makes an appeal.

39 Jesse Stuart in "Thanksgiving Hunter"

It was comfortable to sit on the rock since the sun was directly above me. It warmed me with a glow of autumn. I felt the sun's rays against my face and the sun was good to feel. But the good fresh autumn air was no longer cool as the frost that covered the autumn grass that morning, nor could I feel it go deep into my lungs; the autumn air was warmer and it was flavored more with the scent of pines.

The Writer's Craft

1. Where in this passage does the author appeal to the sense of touch? to the sense of smell? What adjectives does he use in lines 4–5 to describe the autumn air? Which of the five senses dominates this description?

2. In the model, find as many words as you can that appeal to the senses. What impression does the description convey of the narrator's feelings as he warms himself in the sun?

The following description of a forest during and after a thunderstorm is filled with sensory details. Keep in mind the five senses — sight, hearing, touch, smell, and taste. Then as you read the selection, notice to which ones it appeals.

40 Frank Bolles in "A Thunderstorm in the Forest"

For full twenty minutes the trees writhed in the wind, the rain fell, the leaves nodded and shivered under the drops, and the rhythmic roar of the rain was broken irregularly by the thunder. As time passed, the shower slackened, the thunder followed the lightning at longer and longer intervals, the wind seemed to take deeper and less nervous breaths, and I listened to discover what creature of the swamp would first raise its voice above the subsiding storm. A mosquito hovered before me, dodging the drops in its vibratory flight. If it was buzzing, I could not hear it. Suddenly a single call from a blue jay came, in a lull of the wind, from a thicket of spruces. "Yoly-'oly," it said, and was silent again. I took a few steps forward, and the shrill alarm note of a chipmunk sounded through the gloom. I strolled slowly through the drenched and dripping woods fragrant with the perfume of moss and mould. It was more like wading than walking, for every leaf had a drop of cold water ready to give away to whatever first touched it. A ray of sunlight dodged through the lifting clouds and fell into the swamp. The song of a parula warbler, distilled by it, floated back skyward. As the west grew golden and blue, birdsongs sounded from every quarter. The merry chickadees, conversational vireos, and querulous wood pewees vied with each other and the tree toads in replacing the orchestral passion of the storm by the simple music of their solos.

The Writer's Craft

1. To which of the senses does this selection appeal? Across the top of a sheet of paper write the words *sight, hearing, touch,* and *smell.* Then, beneath each word, copy from the model at least one detail appealing to that sense. Compare your list with those of your classmates.

2. A sensory appeal can be made through suggestion. How does "It was more like wading than walking" (lines 20–21) suggest the sense of touch? Explain how the author appeals again to the sense of touch when he writes that "every leaf had a drop of cold water ready to give away to whatever first touched it" (lines 21–22).

Precise verbs play an important part in details that appeal to the sense of sight. What is particularly effective about each of the italicized verbs below?

> For full twenty minutes the trees *writhed* in the wind, the rain fell, the leaves *nodded* and *shivered* under the drops (lines 1–3)
>
> A mosquito *hovered* before me (lines 10–11)
>
> A ray of sunlight *dodged* through the lifting clouds (lines 22–23)

It is important to select sensory details that are appropriate to the speaker and the occasion being described. The following passage describes the sensations of a middle-aged English lady, Mrs. Moore, visiting some famous caves in India, on a tour arranged by her Indian friend Aziz for her and her son's fiancée, Adela.

41 E. M. Forster in *A Passage to India*

A Marabar cave had been horrid as far as Mrs. Moore was concerned, for she had nearly fainted in it, and had some difficulty in preventing herself from saying so as soon as she got into the air again. It was natural enough: she had always suffered from faintness, and the cave had become too full, because all their retinue * followed them. Crammed with villagers and servants, the circular chamber began to smell. She lost Aziz and Adela in the dark, didn't know who touched her, couldn't breathe, and some vile naked thing struck her face and settled on her mouth like a pad. She tried to regain the entrance tunnel, but an influx of villagers swept her back. She hit her head. For an instant

* **retinue:** company.

she went mad, hitting and gasping like a fanatic. For not only did the crush and stench alarm her; there was also a terrifying echo.

The Writer's Craft

1. A cultured English lady is not likely to linger over details that assault the sense of smell. Yet the stench Mrs. Moore refers to can be easily imagined: the heat of India and the stale air of a crowded cave. What details in the selection appeal to the sense of touch? of hearing?

2. The passage makes no appeal to the sense of taste, nor does it contain many details appealing to the sense of sight. Why is the absence of visual details appropriate?

Now You Try It

Select a place or experience in which you were aware of many sense impressions — impressions not only of sight but of the other senses as well. You may, for example, want to choose a scene in a forest like the one described by Frank Bolles, or an experience on a hike or hunting trip in a setting like the one described by Jesse Stuart in Model 39. Thanksgiving dinner, or any similar festivity, will offer a great many sense impressions. A library is a quiet place, but it too appeals to the senses in many ways. A locker room, a drugstore, an airport, a street corner — all are good subjects. Whatever place or experience you choose, describe it in such a way that your reader will experience it through *his* senses.

. . . .

Remember

- *We experience our surroundings through our senses.*
- *Include sensory details to describe a place or an experience vividly.*
- *Sensory details should appeal to as many senses as are appropriate to the occasion being described.*

Narration

LESSON **16**

Writing a Narrative

A narrative is a story. Whether true or imagined, narratives are in general the kind of writing not only most fun to read, but also most fun to write. These next three lessons will help you write interesting and entertaining narratives.

If you were to set down an account of everything that happened to you in the course of one day, you would be writing narration; but such an account would be a story only in a very loose sense. Not everything that happened would be interesting or important. Indeed, many of the day's events would be so commonplace that there would be no point in mentioning them at all. In a well-told story, on the other hand, the writer *selects* from his experiences only those events that he considers interesting or significant.

Every day you yourself make selections of this kind in conversation. In telling how your team won an exciting game, you select details to mention in order to make the strategy clear. One of your teachers was unfair; you saw an accident; something happened that taught you a lesson; a funny incident took place on your way home. For whatever reasons you may later tell someone else about any of those occurrences, you will inevitably select events that illustrate the point you want to make.

In the following narrative, John Steinbeck recounts an experience he had when he and his dog Charley toured the country. Traveling in a truck with a small house built behind the driver's cab, the two of them met with surprises when they reached Yellowstone National Park in Wyoming. As you read, consider whether or not all the events in the narrative illustrate Steinbeck's point in telling the story.

42   John Steinbeck in *Travels with Charley*

[1] I don't know what made me turn sharply south and cross a state line to take a look at Yellowstone. Perhaps it was a fear of my neighbors. I could hear them say, "You mean you were that near to Yellowstone and didn't go? You must be 5 crazy." Again it might have been the American tendency in travel. One goes, not so much to see but to tell afterward. Whatever my purpose in going to Yellowstone, I'm glad I went because I discovered something about Charley I might 10 never have known.

[2] A pleasant-looking National Park man checked me in and then he said, "How about that dog? They aren't permitted in except on leash." 15

[3] "Why?" I asked.

[4] "Because of the bears."

[5] "Sir," I said, "this is a unique dog. He does not live by tooth or fang. He respects the right of cats to be cats although he doesn't admire 20 them. He turns his steps rather than disturb an earnest caterpillar. His greatest fear is that someone will point out a rabbit and suggest that he chase it. This is a dog of peace and tranquility. I suggest that the greatest danger to 25 your bears will be pique * at being ignored by Charley."

[6] The young man laughed. "I wasn't so

* **pique:** resentment.

much worried about the bears," he said. "But our bears have developed an intolerance for dogs. One of them might demonstrate his prejudice with a clip on the chin, and then — no dog."

[7] "I'll lock him in the back, sir. I promise you Charley will cause no ripple in the bear world, and as an old bear-looker, neither will I."

[8] "I just have to warn you," he said. "I have no doubt your dog has the best of intentions. On the other hand, our bears have the worst. Don't leave food about. Not only do they steal but they are critical of anyone who tries to reform them. In a word, don't believe their sweet faces or you might get clobbered. And don't let the dog wander. Bears don't argue."

[9] We went on our way into the wonderland of nature gone nuts, and you will have to believe what happened. The only way I can prove it would be to get a bear.

[10] Less than a mile from the entrance I saw a bear beside the road, and it ambled out as though to flag me down. Instantly a change came over Charley. He shrieked with rage. His lips flared, showing wicked teeth that have some trouble with a dog biscuit. He screeched insults at the bear, which hearing, the bear reared up and seemed to me to overtop Rocinante.* Frantically I rolled the windows shut and, swinging quickly to the left, grazed the animal, then scuttled on while Charley raved and ranted beside me, describing in detail what he would do to that bear if he could get at him. I was never so astonished in my life. To the best of my knowledge Charley had never seen a bear, and in his whole history had showed great tolerance for every living thing. Besides all this,

* **Rocinante:** the name Steinbeck gave to his truck. Originally it was the name of Don Quixote's horse.

Charley is a coward, so deep-seated a coward ⁶⁵ that he has developed a technique for concealing it. And yet he showed every evidence of wanting to get out and murder a bear that outweighed him a thousand to one. I don't understand it. ⁷⁰

[11] A little farther along two bears showed up, and the effect was doubled. Charley became a maniac. He leaped all over me, he cursed and growled, snarled and screamed. I didn't know he had the ability to snarl. Where did he ⁷⁵ learn it? Bears were in good supply, and the road became a nightmare. For the first time in his life, Charley resisted reason, even resisted a cuff on the ear. He became a primitive killer lusting for the blood of his enemy, and up to ⁸⁰ this moment he had had no enemies. In a bearless stretch, I opened the cab, took Charley by the collar, and locked him in the house. But that did no good. When we passed other bears he leaped on the table and scratched at the ⁸⁵ windows, trying to get out at them. I could hear canned goods crashing as he struggled in his mania. Bears simply brought out the Hyde in my Jekyll-headed dog.* What could have caused it? Was it a pre-breed memory of a time ⁹⁰ when the wolf was in him? I know him well. Once in a while he tries a bluff, but it is a palpable ° lie. I swear that this was no lie. I am certain that if he were released, he would have charged every bear we passed and found victory ⁹⁵ or death.

* **the Hyde in my Jekyll-headed dog:** the evil in my innocent-looking dog. In Robert Louis Stevenson's *Dr. Jekyll and Mr. Hyde,* the respectable Dr. Jekyll transforms himself into Mr. Hyde, a vicious criminal. Steinbeck is also punning on "jackal-headed god," an epithet of Anubis, an ancient Egyptian god.
° **palpable:** obvious.

[12] It was too nerve-racking, a shocking spectacle, like seeing an old, calm friend go insane. No amount of natural wonders, of rigid cliffs and belching waters, of smoking springs could even engage my attention while that pandemonium * went on. After about the fifth encounter I gave up, turned Rocinante about, and retraced my way. If I had stopped the night and bears had gathered to my cooking, I dare not think what would have happened.

[13] At the gate the park guard checked me out. "You didn't stay long. Where's the dog?"

[14] "Locked up back there. And I owe you an apology. That dog has the heart and soul of a bear killer and I didn't know it. Heretofore he has been a little tenderhearted toward an underdone steak."

[15] "Yeah!" he said. "That happens sometimes. That's why I warned you. A bear dog would know his chances, but I've seen a Pomeranian go up like a puff of smoke. You know, a well-favored bear can bat a dog like a tennis ball."

[16] I moved fast, back the way I had come, and I was reluctant to camp for fear there might be some unofficial nongovernment bears about. That night I spent in a pretty auto court near Livingston. I had my dinner in a restaurant, and when I had settled in with a drink and a comfortable chair and my bathed bare feet on a carpet with red roses, I inspected Charley. He was dazed. His eyes held a faraway look and he was totally exhausted, emotionally no doubt. He couldn't eat his dinner, he refused the evening walk, and once we were in, he collapsed on the floor and went to sleep. In the night I heard him whining and yapping, and when I turned on the

* **pandemonium:** confusion, noise.

light his feet were making running gestures and his body jerked and his eyes were wide open, [135] but it was only a night bear. I awakened him and gave him some water. This time he went to sleep and didn't stir all night. In the morning he was still tired. I wonder why we think the thoughts and emotions of animals are simple. [140]

The Writer's Craft

1. The last sentence of paragraph 1 states Steinbeck's point in recounting this particular experience. What is that point?

2. The *introduction,* or beginning, of a narrative should arouse the reader's interest; very often it will set the scene. In paragraph 1, how does Steinbeck set the scene? Does he give all the information the reader needs to understand what follows in the narrative? Which sentence in paragraph 1 seems intended to arouse the reader's interest?

3. Throughout the *development* of a narrative, the writer should keep to the point. Does Steinbeck do so throughout this narrative? In other words, is every event he includes related to Charley's reactions to the bears? Might the author also have told about an interesting incident that had occurred the year before when he and his wife toured Europe? Explain your answer.

4. The *conclusion* of a narrative should bring it to a satisfying end; it should not run down like an unwound clock. Reread paragraph 16. Does Steinbeck bring this narrative to a satisfactory end? Does he make some point about what happened? What purpose does the last sentence serve?

5. This account of a dog's reaction to bears could have been far less interesting in the hands of a less gifted writer. A good writer is able to make a narrative entertaining simply by the way he tells it, just as a poor writer telling the same story can make it dull. Have someone in your class read aloud paragraph 5. Is the author exaggerating here? Do you think he really spoke to the National Park man in just those words?

What would have been lost if, instead of writing that paragraph, Steinbeck had written no more than: "'Sir,' I said, 'this is a peaceful dog. He won't bother your bears'"?

6. Reread paragraph 10 and point out places where the author again reveals his sense of humor.

7. A writer can make his experiences even more interesting by setting down the feelings they provoked. In lines 60–61, for example, Steinbeck tells how surprised he was when Charley first went mad: "I was never so astonished in my life." How did he feel after Charley's behavior inside the house (lines 97–99)? after they had left Yellowstone (lines 120–22)?

Now You Try It

1. Write a brief narrative about an experience that did not turn out as you expected it would. The following suggestions may remind you of one you would enjoy writing about.

  a. You have been looking forward to loafing through a holiday. The big day comes, and you find yourself busy from morning to night.
  b. A trip yields plenty of excitement but not in the way you counted on.
  c. Your class presents a one-act play in the school auditorium. As the curtain goes up you *think* you know your part.
  d. A visit to relatives turns out to be different from how you had imagined it.
  e. You think you have reason to dislike your new neighbors, and discover in time that your hunch was right.
  f. Dinner is served. You had a hand in preparing it, and it isn't fit to eat.

After deciding what experience you would like to write about, plan your story. List the separate events that formed the experience, and eliminate those that are not closely related to the point of the story — the point being in this instance that things did not turn out as expected.

2. After you have finished writing, reread your narrative. You should be able to answer *yes* to each of the following questions:

Does the beginning set the scene and arouse the reader's interest?

Is each event you include important to the point of the story?

Have you used precise, carefully chosen words that make the experience seem real?

Have you added to the interest of the story by telling how you felt at different times during the experience you are relating?

Does the conclusion bring the story to a satisfying end?

. . . .

Remember

— *An effective narrative tells a single story.*

— *In an effective narrative, each event is related to the point of the story.*

— *Telling how you felt during an experience makes it more interesting to the reader.*

LESSON **17**

Description in Narration

Most good narrative contains description — of the appearance and actions of characters, of the scenes where certain events occurred, and of any objects that are important to the story. In the following narrative D. H. Lawrence, son of an English coal miner, relates an experience that he might have had during his own boyhood. As you read, notice how descriptions help bring the experience to life.

43 **D. H. Lawrence in "Adolf"**

When we were children, our father often worked on the night shift. Once it was springtime, and he used to arrive home, black and tired, just as we were downstairs in our nightdresses. Then night met morning face to face, ⁵ and the contact was not always happy. Perhaps it was painful to my father to see us gaily entering upon the day into which he dragged himself soiled and weary. He didn't like going to bed in the spring-morning sunshine. ¹⁰

But sometimes he was happy because of his long walk through the dewy fields in the first daybreak. He loved the open morning, the crys-

tal and the space, after a night down pit.* He
watched every bird, every stir in the trembling 15
grass, answered the whinnying of the pewits
and tweeted to the wrens. If he could, he also
would have whinnied and tweeted and whistled
in a native language that was not human. He
liked nonhuman things best. 20

One sunny morning we were all sitting at table when we heard his heavy, slurring walk up
the entry. We became uneasy. His was always a
disturbing presence, trammeling.° He passed
the window darkly, and we heard him go into 25
the scullery and put down his tin bottle. But directly he came into the kitchen. We felt at once
that he had something to communicate. No one
spoke. We watched his black face for a second.

"Give me a drink," he said. 30

My mother hastily poured out his tea. He
went to pour it out into the saucer. But instead
of drinking, he suddenly put something on the
table among the teacups. A tiny brown rabbit!
A small rabbit, a mere morsel, sitting against the 35
bread as still as if it were a made thing.

"A rabbit! A young one! Who gave it you,
Father?"

But he laughed enigmatically,† with a sliding
motion of his yellow-gray eyes, and went to take 40
off his coat. We pounced on the rabbit.

"Is it alive? Can you feel its heart beat?"

My father came back and sat down heavily in
his armchair. He dragged his saucer to him and
blew his tea, pushing out his red lips under his 45
black moustache.

"Where did you get it, Father?"

* **down pit:** in the coal mine.
° **trammeling:** restricting.
† **enigmatically:** mysteriously.

"I picked it up," he said, wiping his naked forearm over his mouth and beard.

"Where?"

"It is a wild one!" came my mother's quick voice.

"Yes, it is."

"Then why did you bring it?" cried my mother.

"Oh, we wanted it," came our cry.

"Yes, I've no doubt you did — " retorted my mother. But she was drowned in our clamor of questions.

On the field path my father had found a dead mother rabbit and three dead little ones — this one alive, but unmoving.

"But what had killed them, Daddy?"

"I couldn't say, my child. I s'd think she'd aten something."

"Why did you bring it!" — again my mother's voice of condemnation. "You know what it will be."

My father made no answer, but we were loud in protest.

"He must bring it. It's not big enough to live by itself. It would die," we shouted.

"Yes, and it will die now. And then there'll be another outcry."

My mother set her face against the tragedy of dead pets. Our hearts sank.

"It won't die, Father, will it? Why will it? It won't."

"I s'd think not," said my father.

"You know well enough it will. Haven't we had it all before!" said my mother.

"They dunna always pine," * replied my father testily.

* **dunna always pine:** do not always weaken and die.

But my mother reminded him of other little wild animals he had brought, which had sulked [85] and refused to live, and brought storms of tears and trouble in our house of lunatics.

Trouble fell on us. The little rabbit sat on our lap, unmoving, its eyes wide and dark. We brought it milk, warm milk, and held it to its [90] nose. It sat still as if it was far away, retreated down some deep burrow, hidden, oblivious. We wetted its mouth and whiskers with drops of milk. It gave no sign, did not even shake off the wet white drops. Somebody began to shed a [95] few secret tears.

"What did I say?" cried my mother. "Take it and put it down in the field."

Her command was in vain. We were driven to get dressed for school. There sat the rabbit. It [100] was like a tiny obscure cloud. Watching it, the emotions died out of our breast. Useless to love it, to yearn over it. Its little feelings were all ambushed. They must be circumvented.* Love and affection were a trespass upon it. A little wild [105] thing, it became more mute and asphyxiated still, in its own arrest, when we approached with love. We must not love it. We must circumvent it for its own existence.

So I passed the order to my sisters and my [110] mother. The rabbit was not to be spoken to, nor even looked at. Wrapping it in a piece of flannel, I put it in an obscure corner of the cold parlor and put a saucer of milk before its nose. My mother was forbidden to enter the parlor while [115] we were at school.

"As if I should take any notice of your nonsense," she cried, affronted. Yet I doubt if she ventured into the parlor.

* **circumvented:** gone around.

At midday, after school, creeping into the [120] front room, there we saw the rabbit still and unmoving in a piece of flannel. Strange gray-brown neutralization of life, still living! It was a sore problem to us. "Why won't it drink its milk, Mother?" we whispered. Our father was [125] asleep.

"It prefers to sulk its life away, silly little thing." A profound problem. Prefers to sulk its life away! We put young dandelion leaves to its nose. The sphinx was not more oblivious. [130] Yet its eye was bright.

At teatime, however, it had hopped a few inches, out of its flannel, and there it sat again, uncovered, a little solid cloud of muteness, brown, with unmoving whiskers. Only its side [135] palpitated slightly with life.

Darkness came; my father set off to work. The rabbit was still unmoving. Dumb despair was coming over the sisters, a threat of tears before bedtime. Clouds of my mother's anger [140] gathered as she muttered against my father's wantonness.*

Once more the rabbit was wrapped in the old pit singlet.° But now it was carried into the scullery and put under the copper fireplace that it [145] might imagine itself inside a burrow. The saucers were placed about, four or five, here and there on the floor, so that if the little creature should chance to hop abroad, it could not fail to come upon some food. After this my mother [150] was allowed to take from the scullery what she wanted and then she was forbidden to open the door.

When morning came and it was light, I went

* **wantonness:** carelessness.
° **pit singlet:** woolen undershirt worn in coal mines.

downstairs. Opening the scullery door, I heard a ¹⁵⁵ slight scuffle. Then I saw dabbles of milk all over the floor and tiny rabbit droppings in the saucers. And there was the miscreant,* the tips of his ears showing behind a pair of boots. I peeped at him. He sat bright-eyed and askance, ¹⁶⁰ twitching his nose and looking at me while not looking at me.

He was alive — very much alive. But still we were afraid to trespass much on his confidence.

"Father!" My father was arrested at the door. ¹⁶⁵ "Father, the rabbit's alive."

"Back your life it is," said my father.

"Mind how you go in."

By evening, however, the little creature was tame, quite tame. He was christened Adolf. We ¹⁷⁰ were enchanted by him. We couldn't really love him, because he was wild and loveless to the end. But he was an unmixed delight.

* **miscreant:** villain.

The Writer's Craft

1. Lines 1–20 are introductory. In those lines, does the author give all the information the reader needs to understand the development of the narrative? In line 20 he states that the father "liked nonhuman things best." Do you think the story demonstrates that characteristic of the father? Explain.

2. Does Lawrence keep to a single point? Explain why he does not relate anything that happened to the children at school or to the mother at home during the day.

3. Reread the final paragraph of the narrative. Does the author bring his story to a satisfactory end? Compare the last two sentences in this narrative with the last sentence in Model 42, by John Steinbeck. Do you see any similarity in the conclusions of the two selections?

4. Lawrence's vivid descriptions are important to the success of this narrative. Although sometimes no longer than a single sentence, they are filled with specific details.

> But he laughed enigmatically, with a sliding motion of his yellow-gray eyes, and went to take off his coat. (lines 39–41)
>
> He dragged his saucer to him and blew his tea, pushing out his red lips under his black moustache. (lines 44–46)
>
> The little rabbit sat on our lap, unmoving, its eyes wide and dark. (lines 88–89)

Glance through the narrative again to find at least two other brief word pictures. Explain why you think they could serve as examples of effective description.

5. Notice that in all of his descriptions Lawrence uses precise nouns and verbs and carefully chosen adjectives. In lines 91–92, for example, he writes that the rabbit "sat still as if it was far away, retreated down some *deep burrow.*" Why would it have been less effective to write that the rabbit "sat still as if it was far away, retreated down some *rabbit hole*"? Notice the author's careful selection of words in the examples below. Explain the effectiveness of the italicized words.

Nouns

> My mother set her face against the *tragedy* of dead pets. (lines 75–76)
>
> *storms* of tears and trouble (lines 86–87)
>
> *despair* was coming over the sisters (lines 138–39)
>
> I saw *dabbles* of milk all over the floor (lines 156–57)

Verbs

> he *dragged* himself (lines 8–9)
>
> We *pounced* on the rabbit. (line 41)
>
> We *wetted* its mouth and whiskers . . . (lines 92–93)
>
> Yet I doubt if she *ventured* into the parlor. (lines 118–19)

Adjectives
> his *heavy,* slurring walk (line 22)
> an *obscure* corner of the *cold* parlor (line 113)
> he was *wild* and *loveless* (line 172)
> But he was an *unmixed* delight (line 173)

6. Descriptions in a well-written story help the reader understand the characters. Do you understand the father in this narrative? Look at some of the adjectives in the first three paragraphs that describe him: *black* and *tired* (lines 3–4), *soiled* and *weary* (line 9), *heavy* and *slurring* (line 22), *disturbing* (line 24), and *trammeling* (line 24). What overall impression of the father do those adjectives convey?

7. In the same three paragraphs Lawrence also creates the impression that the father was a happy man. How? Altogether, would you say that the father is a believable character? Have you ever known anyone who seemed gloomy at times and cheerful at other times? Is such a person the type who might suddenly bring a baby rabbit to the breakfast table?

8. Notice the sensory details in lines 11–20. Does mention of "the dewy fields," "the open morning, the crystal and the space" almost make you *feel* the morning air? In lines 11–20, how does the author appeal to the sense of sight? to the sense of hearing?

9. Adolf is described with fresh, vivid comparisons. When the rabbit is first introduced, Lawrence calls it "a mere morsel, sitting against the bread as still as if it were a made thing" (lines 35–36). Why does he call Adolf a "morsel"? In what way is the rabbit like "a made thing"? Later, the author writes that Adolf was "like a tiny obscure cloud" (line 101). Why is that comparison effective? Find another place in the story where the rabbit is compared to a cloud.

WORD CHOICE: ADVERBS

As you know, adverbs must be used sparingly for best effect. A good writer does not often use a verb-adverb combination, like *talked rapidly,* if a more precise verb, like *chattered,* is available. To test Lawrence's use of adverbs in this narrative, see if you can replace any of the following verb-adverb combinations with a single, more precise verb.

passed . . . darkly (lines 24–25)
hastily poured (line 31)
laughed enigmatically (line 39)
sat . . . heavily (line 43)
replied . . . testily (lines 82–83)
palpitated slightly (line 136)

Now You Try It

1. Write a brief narrative based on a personal experience, bringing it to life by means of description. The task will be easier if you choose an experience that has some color and action in it. Suggestions below may remind you of an experience of your own that would form the basis of an interesting story.

a. You bring home a sick bird or animal.
b. Your father buys a dog.
c. You have a frightening experience — exploring, getting lost, becoming involved in a fight.
d. You and your family visit Grand Canyon.
e. You try door-to-door selling.
f. Your family undertakes a project — landscaping, house painting, cleaning, moving.
g. You decide to stand up to someone who has pushed you around.

2. After you have finished writing the story, reread it and revise wherever necessary. The questions below will guide you in your revision.

Does the beginning give all the information necessary for the reader to follow the development?
Is every event related to the main point of the story?
Are important people, places, and objects described in detail?

Are descriptions made vivid by means of sensory details and fresh comparisons?

Does the conclusion bring the story to a satisfactory end?

. . . .

Remember

- *Most effective narratives contain description.*
- *Description may help the reader understand the characters.*
- *Specific details, sensory details, and fresh comparisons help bring a story to life.*

LESSON **18**

Using Dialogue

Writers have two ways of telling what the characters in a story say to each other. In indirect quotation the writer uses his own words to report the sense of what was said. In direct quotation he quotes the speaker's words exactly.

> *Indirect:* My father asked me why I needed a dollar.
> *Direct:* "Why do you need a dollar?" my father asked.

In a narrative, conversations of characters given as direct quotation are called *dialogue*. If those conversations sound natural, if they are lively as well as interesting, and if they reveal something about the speaker while helping to move the story forward, then the dialogue is wholly successful.

The following narrative tells of the Sunday-afternoon activities of several boys. Notice not only how much of it is in dialogue but also how natural the dialogue sounds.

44 William Saroyan in *The Human Comedy*

After church and Sunday dinner, August Gottlieb was in his front yard patching an old tennis net into something which he hoped might turn out to be useful. Enoch Hopper, a boy of Auggie's age, came by swiftly, stopped ⁵ swiftly, and watched swiftly. He was the owner of an old baseball with the cover gone, which he slammed onto the sidewalk fiercely, making it bounce very high. He caught the ball and slammed it again and again. Enoch Hopper [10] was the most high-strung boy in Ithaca, the most restless, the swiftest-moving, the most impatient, and the loudest-talking.

"What are you making, Auggie?" he said.

"Net," Auggie said. [15]

"What for?" Enoch said. "Fish?"

"No," Auggie said, "animals."

Already Enoch Hopper was bored. "Come on," he said, "let's start a baseball game or go out to Guggenheim's water tank and climb it." [20]

"Got to fix the net," Auggie said.

"Ah, what've you got to fix the net for?" Enoch shouted impatiently.

"Catch animals," Auggie said.

"Where do you see any animals around here?" [25] the high-strung boy said. "Come on, let's go," he shouted. "Let's go out to Malaga and go swimming."

"I'll catch animals in this net all right," Auggie said. [30]

"Couldn't catch a flea with that tennis net," Enoch Hopper said. "Come on, let's start a game. Let's go down and sneak into the Bijou, see a Tarzan picture."

"I'll catch a dog first," Auggie said, "just to [35] test the net — just to see if it works. And then if it *does* work, watch out!"

"Ah, that's an old tennis net," Enoch said. "You won't catch anything with it. Let's go down to the courthouse park, to the city jail, [40] and talk to the prisoners."

"I've got to fix my animal net," Auggie said. "I'm going to try it out today — and if it works — oh, boy — tomorrow!"

"Oh, boy, *what*?" Enoch said. "There's no [45] animals around here. A cow. A couple of dogs.

Six or seven rabbits. A few chickens — what are you going to catch?"

"I got a good net here," Auggie said. "Big enough for a bear."

"Ah, come on, let's go," Enoch said. "What do you want to be fooling with an old tennis net for? Big enough for a bear? You couldn't catch a teddy bear with that net."

"Think a lion could catch *you?*" Auggie asked.

"Naaah," Enoch said, "I'm too fast. A lion couldn't get anywhere near me. Come on, let's go over across the Southern Pacific tracks and get into a game with the Cosmos Playground gang."

"I'll bet you'd be *harder* to catch in a trap than a lion," Auggie said.

"No trap in the world fast enough to catch me," Enoch said. "Let's go out to the fairgrounds and run around the mile track. I'll give you a hundred yards head start."

"I'll bet your own father couldn't catch you," Auggie said.

"Naaah," Enoch said, "couldn't come anywhere near me. I'd leave him in the dust."

Now Lionel came up. "What are you making, Auggie?" he said.

"Net," Auggie said — "to catch animals."

"Couldn't catch a flea with that net, Lionel," Enoch said. "Come on, let's go out on the empty lot and play catch. How about it?"

"*Me?*" Lionel said.

"Sure, Lionel," Enoch said. "Come on. You throw 'em to me real hard. I'll throw 'em to you real easy. Come on, come on, half the afternoon's gone."

"All right, Enoch," Lionel said, "but remember — throw 'em easy. I ain't so good at catch.

Sometimes I miss and the ball hits me in the 85
face. Hurt my eyes once, my nose twice."

"I'll throw 'em easy. Don't worry," Enoch
said. "Come on, come on."

Enoch Hopper and Lionel Cabot moved
across the street to the empty lot and Auggie 90
went back to his work. Soon he had all of the
pieces of the old tennis net sewn together so
that there was an almost square piece of netting. He stretched this netting out and attached
each corner to a stick in the ground so that he 95
could behold what he had made. Now Shag
Manoogian came over the backyard fence to
Auggie. "What's that?" he said.

"Net," Auggie said — "to catch animals.
Want to help me try it out?" 100

"Sure," Shag said. "How are you going to do
it?"

"Well," Auggie said, "I'll hold the net and
hide here behind Ara's store. You call Enoch.
He's over there playing catch with Lionel. 105
Enoch is swifter and harder to catch than a
lion. If this net can hold Enoch, it can hold
anything. All right. I'm hiding. I'm ready. Call
Enoch. Tell him you want to ask him something." 110

"OK," Shag said. He looked over at Enoch
on the empty lot and then called out very loud,
"Enoch! Oh, Enoch!"

Enoch Hopper turned and shouted back,
twice as loud, "What do you want, Shag?" 115

"Come here, Enoch," Shag shouted. "I want
to ask you something."

"What do you want to ask me?" Enoch
shouted.

"I'll tell you when you get here," Shag 120
shouted.

"OK," Enoch shouted, and started running toward Shag, with Lionel following but not quite sure whether he should run or walk.

"All right, Shag," Auggie whispered. "Duck [125] back here and hide with me. Take hold of this end of the net. When he comes around the corner of the store, we'll jump on him and capture him. See?"

Running swiftly, Enoch shouted, "Let's go [130] out to Malaga and go swimming. Half the afternoon's gone already. Let's do something. What are we waiting for?"

Enoch came running around the corner of Mr. Ara's market. Auggie and Shag leaped out [135] swiftly and spread the net over him. Sure enough, Enoch Hopper moved like a wild undomesticated animal, perhaps a lion. The two big-game hunters worked furiously but the net was not quite strong enough, and soon Enoch [140] Hopper was standing upright, completely unoffended and very much interested in the outcome of the test.

He slammed the baseball on the sidewalk. "Come on, Auggie," he shouted, "let's go! That [145] net couldn't catch a flea! Come on! What are we waiting for?"

"OK," Auggie said, and threw the net into the yard. "Let's go to the courthouse park and talk to the prisoners." [150]

Auggie, Enoch, Shag, and, not far behind them, Lionel moved on down the street toward the courthouse park. Soon Enoch Hopper was a block ahead of the others, shouting back at them, "Come on! Hurry up! What are you mov- [155] ing so slow for?" He threw the baseball at a bird which had come down in a tree, but missed it.

The Writer's Craft

1. The very first sentence sets the scene. When and where does this narrative take place? Does the first sentence serve also to arouse the reader's interest? Explain.

2. Does Saroyan's dialogue sound realistic? Do you think boys actually talk the way the boys in this story do? Because most people use incomplete sentences in their everyday conversations, realistic dialogue often contains sentence fragments. Compare example A with example B below:

A   "What are you making, Auggie?" he said.
          "Net," Auggie said.
          "What for?" Enoch said. "Fish?"
          "No," Auggie said, "animals."

B   "What are you making, Auggie?" he said.
          "I am making a net," Auggie said.
          "What are you making a net for?" Enoch said. "Are you making it to catch fish?"
          "No," Auggie said, "I am making it to catch animals."

Obviously, Saroyan's dialogue (example A) sounds more natural. Why does example B sound unnatural? In the model, find three examples of sentence fragments or single-word statements used effectively in dialogue.

3. Slang and contractions (*I'm* for *I am; couldn't* for *could not*) are two marks of informal language. Notice that the following dialogue from the model is in the language of everyday speech:

> "Think a lion could catch *you?*" Auggie asked.
>
> "Naaah," Enoch said, "I'm too fast. A lion couldn't get anywhere near me. Come on, let's go over across the Southern Pacific tracks and get into a game with the Cosmos Playground gang."
>
> "I'll bet you'd be *harder* to catch in a trap than a lion," Auggie said.

Now reread lines 79–88 and explain why the informal language in those lines constitutes effective, natural dialogue. Does the passage convey the natural rhythms of speech?

4. Speeches in realistic dialogue are usually brief. In this narrative, for example, most of the speeches are only one to three lines long. Why does dialogue so often consist of short speeches?

5. Frequently dialogue that is effective reveals something about the speaker. For instance, one of Enoch Hopper's first remarks is: " 'Come on . . . let's start a baseball game or go out to Guggenheim's water tank and climb it.' " On the basis of that speech, what sort of person do you think Enoch is? He makes similar speeches elsewhere in the narrative. Find three other examples.

6. Effective dialogue helps advance the story. Saroyan, in fact, tells almost all of this narrative through dialogue. Speeches let the reader know what the characters are doing, what they are planning, what they are thinking. Read again the following speech:

> "Well," Auggie said, "I'll hold the net and hide here behind Ara's store. You call Enoch. He's over there playing catch with Lionel. Enoch is swifter and harder to catch than a lion. If this net can hold Enoch, it can hold anything. All right. I'm hiding. I'm ready. Call Enoch. Tell him you want to ask him something."

Explain how the author moves the narrative forward with that speech. How else might he have done so? What advantages are there in advancing a story through dialogue?

7. In using dialogue the writer must make clear who is speaking, and often he must also tell how the person speaks. He can do both with an expression like "Enoch Hopper shouted back." Such identifications are called *dialogue tags*, and some writers work hard to vary the form they take throughout a narrative. That is, instead of using "he said," "I said," "she said" throughout the story, they prefer to use many different tags, such as "he exclaimed," "Mother replied," "I whispered." But do you think a writer could use too many different tags, thereby detracting from the dialogue rather than improving it? Glance through the model again. Does Saroyan spoil his dialogue by trying too hard for variety in the tags? Explain your answer.

8. In a good story the reader is eager to find out what happens next. Early in this narrative, Saroyan arouses his reader's curiosity about the net. Gradually he plants the idea that the net may be used on Enoch, restless, swift, and uncatchable. Until the reader finds out whether or not a capture of Enoch is made, he is kept in suspense. At what point in the story do you first begin to feel suspense? At what point does Saroyan relieve it?

Now You Try It

Write a story in which the events are told principally through dialogue. One of the following suggestions may remind you of an experience of your own that would make a good story.

a. Some boys and girls decide to surprise a friend — perhaps at a party. (Through dialogue let your reader know what plan they work out; then show whether or not it succeeds.)

b. At half time you and your teammates devise a strategy that you think will win the game. (Reveal the strategy through dialogue; then let the reader see how it actually works out.)

c. Several boys or girls make something and try it out — a "soapbox" car, a tent, a costume, a rocket, a raft, a home movie. (Reveal the principal events of the story through dialogue.)

d. Some friends decide to play a practical joke on one of their number in the hope of teaching him a lesson or improving his manners. (Use dialogue to develop the situation and to reveal certain things about the personalities of the characters.)

Before writing the story, review the rules for using quotation marks and other punctuation in dialogue. As you write, try to use dialogue purposefully. It should either advance the story or reveal something important about the speaker. The best dialogue will do both. And it must sound natural;

in other words, like real speech it should include incomplete sentences, contractions, and slang where appropriate. Begin a new paragraph every time the speaker changes.

....

Remember

- *Dialogue should sound natural.*
- *Effective dialogue reveals something about the speaker and helps advance the story.*

Exposition

LESSON **19**
Developing a Topic

Exposition deals with ideas. When your purpose in writing is to report on something or to explain something to your reader or to inform or convince him of something, what you are writing is exposition.

In exposition you develop a topic by giving information. To make the information clear and understandable, you must organize your writing carefully. What organization is appropriate? It depends on your topic and on the kind of information with which you plan to develop it. The important thing is that you organize the whole composition *logically*, so that your reader will be able to follow the way it proceeds.

In the next model, the writer begins with a topic, or controlling idea. Watch how she develops the topic with carefully organized information.

45   Pat Hunt in "Life Patterns of Baboons"

[1] Life among baboons takes a regular, predictable pattern. Each troop lives in an area of about fifteen square miles. At night they climb into the trees to sleep in an upright position, sitting comfortably on their well-padded rumps, ready to flee at the slightest crackle that betrays a raiding

lion or cheetah. At dawn they descend to the ground for the day.

[2] As they move across the plains, within range of trees if possible, the troop falls into a standard formation. Leading are strong young males. Then come females and juveniles. In the center of the troop are the dominant males and the females with infants. This is the core of the troop, the part that must be protected if the troop is to survive. Behind the core come more juveniles and unattached males and females. A couple of young males may range out as scouts at the sides of the column. If a predator is sighted, the whole troop makes for the nearest trees — except for the leader and his main supporters. These step forward to meet the danger head on and protect the retreat. Two or three baboons can bluff or fight off a cheetah until the rest are well away. Occasionally on the march a female with a newborn infant temporarily drops back, and when she does, one of the major males also drops back to walk beside her till she can keep up. A solitary baboon is a dead baboon; survival is possible only within the group.

[3] The new infants are the main concern of the troop. A mother never lets her baby out of grabbing distance, and when she walks, it rides slung under her belly. After four months a baby graduates to its mother's back, later sitting upright and riding jockey style. All the while it learns what to eat by watching her pull up new shoots of grass or dig for the stems and roots, being careful to knock off the dirt before chewing — it saves a lot of wear and tear on the teeth.

[4] After a year a juvenile grows more independent of its mother and spends more time with baboons its own age. Here the male gets his schooling, developing his physical strength and skill. And here he learns how to get along with other

baboons, working out his place in the baboon hierarchy. Separated by now from his mother, he is subject to discipline from the leading males, who bite his rump if he gets out of line. As long as a female is caring for an infant, she is a privileged member of the troop, waited on by males and other females. Once the baby has grown away from her, she is relegated to the ranks.

The Writer's Craft

1. The author states her topic, or controlling idea, in the first sentence: "Life among baboons takes a regular, predictable pattern." Throughout the rest of the selection, does she develop that topic fully? Judging from this model, where is the topic stated in a well-organized explanation? Why?

2. To develop her topic, the author follows a logical plan here. In paragraph 1 she explains where baboons live and where they sleep. In paragraph 2 she writes about the "standard formation" into which they fall as they travel across the plains. Beginning with the "strong young males" who lead, she discusses the rest of the formation in order. Which members of the troop does she introduce with the following transitional expressions?

Then . . .
In the center . . .
Behind . . .

Notice that in the same paragraph she goes on to mention exceptions to the standard formation. Where in paragraph 2 does she tell what happens when one of the mothers falls back? She could hardly have begun the paragraph with that exception and then gone on to describe the standard formation. Why would such a plan have been confusing?

3. In paragraphs 3 and 4, does the writer continue to develop the topic stated in the beginning? In those paragraphs, find three facts or examples showing that life among baboons assumes a regular pattern.

4. If you were to outline the plan followed in the model, it might look like this:

Topic: Life among baboons takes a regular, predictable pattern
  I. Where they live, sleep
  II. How they travel across plains
  III. How they care for infants
  IV. How youngsters become independent of mothers

Does the outline seem to provide a clear and logical plan for presenting the relevant information? Explain.

5. When specific, information is valuable and interesting. Reread paragraph 3 and compare it with the version below.

> The new infants are the main concern of the troop. A mother always keeps her baby close to her. When she walks, she carries it. She also teaches the baby what to eat and how to eat it.

Why is the original paragraph more informative and interesting than the rewritten version?

6. In exposition, paragraph structure is especially important. In the paragraphs in this selection, where do the topic sentences usually appear? Do you think they are in the most effective position? Explain your answer.

7. Does the writer give enough facts and examples in each paragraph to develop her topic sentences fully?

8. Unity is as important in a composition as it is in a paragraph. Is this model unified? That is, does every paragraph help develop the writer's topic, or controlling idea?

Now You Try It

1. Write an expository composition of 250–350 words in which you develop a topic by giving information. The following suggestions may help you think of a suitable topic:

  a. Life at home follows a routine.
  b. A junior high school student can have a crowded daily schedule.

c. During vacations my life assumes a simple (or complicated) pattern.
d. This part of the country is rich in natural wonders.
e. Our town has many places of historic interest.
f. Discrimination leads to suffering and injustice.
g. My father's job requires skill.
h. Movies can be educational.

Before beginning to write, organize your ideas in a simple outline like the one given on page 136 for Model 45. (Later you will hand in that outline with your composition.)

As you write, remember to develop the topic with specific information. Use facts and examples to support the topic sentences of your paragraphs, and when necessary use transitional expressions to keep the piece moving forward smoothly.

2. Afterward, reread the composition to be sure that it is unified and clear. Revise wherever you can improve your work.

....

Remember

— *In general, state the topic of an expository composition in the first paragraph.*
— *Give specific information to develop the topic.*
— *Organize your writing to present the information clearly.*

LESSON **20**

Explaining a Process

Explaining a process means explaining how something is done or how something works. A home economics teacher telling how to prepare a balanced meal and a scientist writing about how a new rocket functions are both engaged in explaining a process. In undertaking such an explanation yourself, you should first divide the process into a number of steps. Then you can proceed to explain the entire operation step by step from the beginning.

To learn how to proceed, read the following selection, which explains how to put up a tent on an overnight camping trip.

46   Stewart Edward White in "On Making Camp"

[1] When five or six o'clock draws near, begin to look about you for a good, level, dry place, elevated some few feet above the surroundings. Drop your pack or beach your canoe. Examine the location carefully. You will want two trees about ten feet apart, from which to suspend your tent, and a bit of flat ground underneath them. Of course the flat ground need not be particularly unencumbered by brush or saplings, so the combination ought not to be hard to discover.

[2] With the little ax, clear the ground thoroughly. By bending a sapling over strongly with the left hand, clipping sharply at the strained fibers, and then bending it as strongly the other way to repeat the ax stroke on the other side, you will find that treelets of even two or three inches diameter can be felled by two blows. In a very few moments, you will have accomplished a hole in the forest, and your two supporting trees will stand sentinel at either end of a most respectable-looking clearing.

[3] Now, although the ground seems free of all but unimportant growths, go over it thoroughly for little shrubs and leaves. They look soft and yielding, but are often possessed of unexpectedly abrasive roots. Besides, they mask the face of the ground. When you have finished pulling them up by the roots, you will find that your supposedly level plot is knobby with hummocks. Stand directly over each little mound; swing the back of your ax vigorously against it, adz-wise,* between your legs. Nine times out of ten it will crumble, and the tenth time means merely a root to cut or a stone to pry out. At length you are possessed of a plot of clean, fresh earth, level and soft, free from projections.

[4] Lay a young birch or maple an inch or so in diameter across a log. Two clips ° will produce you a tent peg. If you are inexperienced, and cherish memories of striped lawn marquees, you will cut them about six inches long. If you are wise and old and gray in woods experience, you will multiply that length by four. Then your loops will not slip off, and you will have a real grip on mother earth, than which nothing can be more desirable in the event of a heavy rain and wind squall about mid-

* **adz-wise:** used like an adz, a small cutting tool.
° **clips:** strokes of the ax.

night. If your ax is as sharp as it ought to be, you can point them more neatly by holding them suspended in front of you while you snip at their ends with the ax, rather than by resting them against a solid base. Pile them together at the edge of the clearing. Cut a crotched sapling eight or ten feet long. Now unpack your tent.

[5] In a wooded country you will not take the time to fool with tent poles. A stout line run through the eyelets and along the apex will string it successfully between your two trees. Draw the line as tight as possible, but do not be too unhappy if, after your best efforts, it still sags a little. That is what your long crotched stick is for. Stake out your four corners. If you get them in a good rectangle and in such relation to the apex as to form two isosceles triangles of the ends, your tent will stand smoothly. Therefore, be an artist and do it right. Once the corners are well placed, the rest follows naturally. Occasionally, in the North Country, it will be found that the soil is too thin, over the rocks, to grip the tent pegs. In that case drive them at a sharp angle as deep as they will go and then lay a large flat stone across the slant of them. Thus anchored, you will ride out a gale. Finally, wedge your long sapling crotch under the line — outside the tent, of course — to tighten it. Your shelter is up. If you are a woodsman, ten or fifteen minutes has sufficed to accomplish all this.

The Writer's Craft

1. The explanation of a process is usually organized in chronological order. This model begins, "When five or six o'clock draws near . . ." and ends, "ten or fifteen minutes has sufficed to accomplish all this." Is the selection organized chronologically? That is, does the author present each step in the order of its occurrence?

2. The author uses transitional expressions to make his explanation clear. Some of these are *in a very few moments* (paragraph 2), *now* and *when you have finished* (paragraph 3). What transitional word in paragraph 4 tells when the tent should be unpacked? In paragraph 5, what transitional word introduces the last step in the process?

3. Setting up a tent is a complicated operation. To explain it clearly, the author has divided the process into steps and then grouped the steps into four main stages:

Stage one, paragraph 1
Stage two, paragraphs 2–3
Stage three, paragraph 4
Stage four, paragraph 5

After rereading the selection, devise a title for each of the four stages. For example, you might call the first stage *Finding a Location*.

4. To be effective, the explanation of a process must contain specific directions. Notice how many specific directions are given here for each stage in erecting a tent. For example, in paragraph 1 the reader learns that the location he selects must be level, dry, and elevated, and that it must contain two trees separated by about ten feet of flat ground. Find at least three other places in the model that furnish particularly specific directions.

5. In reading the model, did you get the impression that the author is experienced in setting up a tent? To write an explanation of how to do something, should the writer have done the thing himself? Give reasons for your answer.

6. When explaining how to do something, you can help your reader by foreseeing some of the problems he may encounter or the mistakes he may make. For example, White knows it is unlikely that anyone will find a patch of ground free of saplings and bushes. Accordingly, he devotes two paragraphs to telling how to clear and smooth the ground. Reread paragraph 4 and find a place where the author anticipates a mistake the reader may make. What advice does he give?

Now You Try It

Write a composition of 250–350 words in which you explain a process. The process should be one with which you are quite familiar so that you can explain it clearly to someone else. You might want to explain how to do one of the following:

a. Prepare soil and plant a garden
b. Wash and polish a car
c. Organize a club
d. Clean house
e. Amuse children
f. Keep yourself physically fit
g. Raise a prize-winning animal
h. Make a coffee table, mailbox, birdhouse, model boat, dress, or stew.

If the process you are explaining is complicated, group the steps into stages so that the whole explanation will be understandable. In addition, remember to use transitional expressions wherever necessary to indicate the sequence of the steps.

. . . .

Remember

— *Explain a process by presenting a series of steps in chronological order.*
— *The explanation should contain specific directions.*
— *Anticipate your reader's problems and tell him how to meet them.*

LESSON **21**

Description in Exposition

Description, narration, and exposition are often combined within a single composition. You already know that narration usually contains some description. Similarly, in expository writing there may be both description and narration. In other words, even though your purpose in a composition is expository — to explain or inform — what you write may include description and narration.

The following selection is expository. To develop his topic, however, the author *describes* some underwater sounds that are particularly noticeable because of the silence around them. As you read, be alert to his vivid descriptions of those sounds.

47   J. Y. Cousteau in *The Silent World*

The sea is a most silent world. I say this deliberately on long accumulated evidence and aware that wide publicity has recently been made on the noises of the sea. Hydrophones have recorded clamors that have been sold as ⁵ phonographic curiosa, but the recordings have been grossly amplified. It is not the reality of the sea as we have known it with naked ears. There are noises underwater, very interesting ones that the sea transmits exceptionally well, but a diver [10] does not hear boiler factories.

An undersea sound is so rare that one attaches great importance to it. The creatures of the sea express fear, pain, and joy without audible comment. The old round of life and death passes si- [15] lently, save among the mammals — whales and porpoises. The sea is unaffected by man's occasional uproars of dynamite and ships' engines. It is a silent jungle, in which the diver's sounds are keenly heard — the soft roar of exhalations, [20] the lisp of incoming air, and the hoots of a comrade. One's hunting companion may be hundreds of yards away out of sight, but his missed harpoons may be clearly heard clanging on the rocks, and when he returns one may taunt him [25] by holding up a finger for each shot he missed.

Attentive ears may occasionally perceive a remote creaking sound, especially if the breath is held for a moment. The hydrophone can, of course, swell this faint sound to a din, helpful [30] for analysis — but not the way it sounds to the submerged ear. We have not been able to adduce a theory to explain the creaking sounds. Syrian fishermen select fishing grounds by putting their heads down into their boats to the focal [35] point of the sound shell that is formed by the hull. Where they hear creaking sounds they cast nets. They believe that the sound somehow emanates from rocks below, and rocks mean fish pasturage. Some marine biologists suppose the [40] creaking sound comes from thick thousands of tiny shrimps, scraping pincers in concert. Such a shrimp in a specimen jar will transmit audible snaps. But the Syrians net fish, not shrimps. When we dived into creaking areas, we never [45] found a single shrimp. The distant rustle seems stronger in calm seas after a storm, but this is not always the case. The more we experience the sea, the less certain we are of conclusions.

Some fish can croak like frogs. At Dakar I [50] swam in a loud orchestration of these monotonous animals. Whales, porpoises, croakers, and whatever makes the creaking noise are the only exceptions we know to the silence of the sea.

The Writer's Craft

1. Cousteau's expository purpose here is to give accurate information about the sounds of the sea, in order to disprove false claims often made about undersea noises. Why is describing individual sounds heard underwater a natural way to prove his point?

2. In the second paragraph the author describes the sounds divers make. Find words and phrases with which he describes the following:

the diver's exhalations (line 20)
his inhalations, or the incoming air (line 21)
the noises made by a comrade (lines 21–22)
the sound of harpoons striking rocks (line 24)

Do those words and phrases appeal to your sense of hearing? Which of them seem especially well chosen?

3. What underwater sound does the author describe in his third paragraph (lines 27–49)? in his last paragraph?

WORD CHOICE: NOUNS

Precise nouns help make this description clear and exact. Explain how the precision of the following nouns increases the effectiveness of the description:

clamors (line 5)
uproars (line 18)
harpoons (line 24)
din (line 30)
hull (line 37)
orchestration (line 51)

Now You Try It

Write an expository paragraph of 100–150 words that develops an idea at least partly through description. You may begin with one of the following statements or with one of your own.

  a. A happy family is a noisy family.
  b. Circus performers are people of great courage.
  c. Simplicity is the word for proper school dress.
  d. Growing up in a slum can warp a person's life.
  e. Football is a better game to watch than play.
  f. A movie can change your way of seeing things.

· ·

Remember

— *Exposition often contains description.*
— *Effective description depends on sensory details and carefully chosen words.*

LESSON **22**

Narration in Exposition

In exposition, narration can be used to illustrate or support the writer's ideas. Indeed, sometimes a brief incident is more effective than a long explanation, because it makes the point in a memorable way. For example, if you were writing an expository composition about the need for more playgrounds in your community, you would probably point out that playing in streets is dangerous. One way of supporting that assertion would be by relating an incident about a friend who was playing in the street and was seriously hurt by a car. The incident, of course, would take the form of a narrative.

In the following expository model, Leonard Hall writes about a young Irish setter named Tiger Kilkelly. In the beginning of the selection the author explains that he enjoys watching Tiger because he is developing into a fine bird dog. The point is illustrated by means of narration. Notice how incidents support the ideas expressed in the first paragraph.

48 Leonard Hall in "Lively Adventures"

[1] Young Tiger Kilkelly, the Irish-setter pup, is a source of constant entertainment. Often I have heard it said that the big red Irishmen are hard-

headed, capricious, and difficult to train; that they seldom make a bird dog until they are four years old; and that in breeding them for bench and show, breeders have largely killed their noses and hunting instinct. But this is not true of our old Mike, and, from all the signs, it isn't going to be true of the young dog. He grows like a weed and, from all I know of the Irish-setter type, is developing into a fine animal. He is fast as a greyhound and seems to have a natural nose and hunting instinct. He takes to water like a duck and retrieves everything from butterflies, which he catches on the wing, to rubber boots that are carelessly left within his reach. He is as full of energy and enthusiasm as a boy just out of school, yet learns to mind in a remarkably short time.

[2] When our grandson Ricky was visiting recently, he and I noticed the pup lying out in the yard, gazing intently at some small object between his front paws, which he made no attempt to touch. Suddenly the object moved and Tiger jumped a foot in the air in surprise, then immediately lay down with the thing between his paws and his nose an inch or two away. At first we thought it must be a garden toad; then we heard a wren fussing on the fence close-by. I called to the pup and he came to me, although reluctantly. Leaving him for Ricky to hold, I went and picked up a baby wren — entirely untouched and unharmed — and deposited it in a nearby brush pile. After that we hiked out to the field to see some calves, and Tiger went along willingly. But an hour later, when we had forgotten the incident, we discovered the pup lying out beside the brush pile, gazing intently into it. He had found the baby wren again, though now it was safely out of reach and almost ready to fly.

[3] Down in the bottom fields near the Big Pond, some weeks ago, we discovered a young blue goose grazing with the cattle. Evidently injured, so that it cannot fly, it can run like a streak and thus far has been able to avoid ending up as a meal for a fox. On one occasion, when I was working nearby in the field, I saw Tiger swimming round and round in the pond after the goose. It was an unequal contest, for whenever the pup came too near, the bird would dive. Then Tiger would tread water, turning his head in every direction until the goose appeared again; whereupon the pup would go after it again until I was afraid he would drown from exhaustion. We hurried to the pond and called Tiger, who at once gave up the pursuit and swam over to us. But on one other occasion, when he discovered the goose on a much smaller pond in a clump of trees, he caught it and held on without hurting it, then let it go and came to me when I called.

[4] The box tortoises that wander the fields and woods in large numbers at this season seem to intrigue the bird-dog pup. One day, when I was working in this same field, I saw Tiger heading for the little pond with some large object in his mouth. He waded out neck-deep and dropped it, then went back to ranging the field. Next time I looked, he was heading for the pond again and went through the same performance. The third time this happened I climbed down from the tractor and hurried over to see what it was all about. Tiger came carrying a huge box tortoise. He waded out into the pond, opened his mouth, dropped the tortoise into the water, and headed for the field again. Fortunately for the tortoise, it can swim — or at least float.

[5] Tiger occasionally provides a good laugh by

flushing a cottontail, starting after it like a streak of lightning and then running right over the rabbit without ever seeing it. Yards farther on he will suddenly realize that there is no longer any rabbit scent in his nose and circle back to start over again. Once or twice I have seen him actually catch his rabbit, which startled him so that he at once let go of it; whereupon the quarry picked itself up and made for the safety of the nearest brush pile or groundhog burrow.

[6] Now and then I read about fishing dogs, and I have no doubt that with a little training Tiger could be taught to retrieve fish. Every time we are near the creek, he goes fishing. His favorite method is to corner a bunch of minnows in the shallow water at the head of a riffle * — and then he goes nearly wild with excitement. He tries to step on them or to catch them in his mouth, often tumbling head over heels and getting a good ducking for his efforts. And he will keep this up for a half hour at a time, never discouraged by the fact that so far he has not caught a fish.

* **riffle:** a stretch of shallow, choppy water.

The Writer's Craft

1. The first paragraph states that Tiger "is a source of constant entertainment" and that he "is developing into a fine animal." Does the author support those assertions in the rest of the selection? Does he rely mainly on description, narration, or exposition to develop his ideas? Why is his use of narration effective? How do the incidents show both that Tiger is entertaining and that he is becoming a fine bird dog?

2. The second half of paragraph 1 makes several points about Tiger. Stated in condensed form, those points are as follows:

  a. Tiger is fast.
  b. He seems to have a natural nose and hunting instinct.

c. He takes to water like a duck.

d. He retrieves everything.

e. He is full of energy and enthusiasm.

f. He learns to mind in a short time.

To support those points, the author relates a number of incidents, or short narratives, about Tiger. Reread the model and explain how each incident illustrates one or more of the points in the above list.

3. Notice that events in the narratives are arranged in chronological order. Transitional expressions introduce the narratives and also indicate the time order of events. In paragraph 2, for example, the author uses the expressions *immediately, at first, then, after that,* and *an hour later.* In the model, find at least six other transitional expressions that introduce a narrative or indicate time order.

4. This selection demonstrates that in expository writing you can often use narratives to convey your meaning. Although made up largely of narration, the model is nevertheless considered to be an example of exposition. Why? What is Hall's purpose? Does he accomplish it? Explain your answer.

Now You Try It

Select a topic to develop in a short expository composition. In writing the composition, develop the topic at least partly through narration. Topics below may be helpful as suggestions.

a. About some things, animals have more sense than people.

b. A little brother (or sister) can be a big responsibility.

c. Sometimes the worst thing about homework is trying to do it at home.

d. Summer vacations can be profitable.

e. Luck is sometimes more important than skill.

f. A policeman can be a welcome sight.

....

Remember

- *In an expository composition you can illustrate your ideas by telling a story.*
- *A well-told narrative may be more effective than a long explanation.*

LESSON **23**

Supporting an Opinion

In conversation you probably express your opinion a great many times, and about a great many things:

> "This is a perfect day for apple-picking."
> "I love winter."
> "That book is dull beyond belief."

If you want to convince your listener that your opinion is a sound one, you proceed to explain why you feel as you do; that is, you give reasons to support the opinion.

Compositions based on opinions follow the same procedure. Here, for example, James Michener expresses an opinion about Japan, then gives reasons to support it.

49 **James Michener in "Why I Like Japan"**

[1] Japan pleases me mightily because it is so lovely to look at. Its panorama of beauty is so varied, and the movement from one amazing scene to another so quickly taken, that my eye is constantly charmed.

[2] Rise early and see the mists of morning tenderly creeping away from the rice fields that stretch out from every sleepy village. Stand on some hillside at midday and see the thousand rural workers fanning out over the fields, toiling end-

lessly in the shadow of some magnificent mountain. Walk along some curving beach at nightfall and see the moon coming up against ageless pine trees.

[3] Nowhere is the beauty of the seas so inescapable as here. Sometimes the mountains rush down and plunge their precipices into the pounding surf. Elsewhere the sea creeps silently into some glorious bay fringed by lamplit fishing villages. No matter where you travel in Japan, the cold, gray sea of winter and the pastel oceans of summer are near at hand.

[4] As for the mountains, they are the dominant beauty of Japan. On them tall pines grow and deer flourish. Down their sides torrential streams plummet, bearing silt, and as soon as the merest fragment of land begins to collect along their banks, hundreds of human beings cluster and chop out tiny fields. Here is where the rice paddies begin, and as the mountain bases flatten out into substantial fields, millions of men quickly accumulate, taking strength, as it were, from the mountains.

[5] Of Mount Fuji, the queen of all mountains, little new can be said. Some artists have spent their lives contemplating its serene majesty, but none has completely captured the wonder of this perfect volcano. Its gently sloping sides and irregular snowy cap are exactly as they would be if one set out to draw the world's ideal mountain, and the varied aspects in which Fuji can be seen contribute to this unearthly quality.

The Writer's Craft

1. Michener expresses his opinion in the first sentence: "Japan pleases me mightily because it is so lovely to look at." Does his second sentence express a different opinion, or does

it make the first statement clearer? In the rest of the selection, does the author support the first statement or the second or both?

2. As you know, an opinion is supported by means of reasons, which may be either examples or incidents. Here, the author supports his opinion by giving specific examples of Japan's loveliness. In paragraph 2 he describes the beauty of Japan in the morning, at noon, and at night. What examples of Japan's beauty does he give in the rest of the selection?

3. Do you think examples provide adequate support for the opinion stated in the model? In other words, does the selection as a whole make the statements in the first paragraph convincing?

4. To be convincing, the reasons that support an opinion should be specific. Reread paragraph 2 in the model and compare it with the following rewritten version:

> Rise early and see how lovely Japan is in the morning. At midday, watch all the rural workers toiling. That too can be lovely. At night, see how beautiful Japan is when the moon comes up.

Which paragraph is more convincing? Why?

5. Reread paragraph 1. As you have already noticed, the author's opinion is not only that Japan is beautiful but also that its beauty is varied. Explain how each paragraph shows that the beauty of the country is varied. Why is the last sentence in the model a good conclusion?

6. Is the selection unified? That is, does every paragraph help support the writer's opinion, which is the controlling idea?

WORD CHOICE: VERBS

Notice Michener's choice of precise verbs throughout this model. In paragraph 3, what verbs tell how the mountains slope down to the sea and how the sea moves into the bay? In paragraph 4, find at least three examples of carefully chosen precise verbs. Explain their effectiveness.

Now You Try It

Write a brief composition in which you begin with an opinion and go on to support it with specific reasons. The following statements of opinion might suggest one you can support convincingly.

    a. The American West is well worth seeing.
    b. Every boy should be required to take a course in shop.
    c. Every girl should learn to sew.
    d. Team sports are harder to play than individual sports.
    e. A foreign-language course should be required of every student in junior high school.
    f. Having chores to do around the house teaches a young person responsibility.

. . . .

Remember

    — *In a composition supporting an opinion, the opinion is usually stated at the beginning.*
    — *Support the opinion by giving your reasons for holding it.*
    — *To be persuasive, reasons should be specific.*

Index of Writers

Adams, Thomas E., 76
Alcott, Louisa May, 64
Alpers, Antony, 32
Anderson, Marian, 31
Barrow, George, 46
Bates, Marston, 59
Benedict, Ruth, 36
Bolles, Frank, 96
Bracken, Peg, 69
Branley, Franklyn M., 37
Cather, Willa, 84
Catton, Bruce, 41
Chapman, John L., 51
Coffin, R. P. Tristram, 22
Cousteau, J. Y., 143
Crow, John A., 83
Darrow, Floyd L., 49
Day, Clarence, 57
Durrell, Gerald, 52
Eiseley, Loren, 70
Forbes, Kathryn, 3
Forster, E. M., 98
Gallico, Paul, 33
Galsworthy, John, 65
Gardner, John W., 24

Hall, Leonard, 147
Hawthorne, Nathaniel, 92
Hersey, John, 81
Hunt, Pat, 133
Kahan, Stanley, 44
Kelly, Walt, 13
Kieran, John, 6
Lawrence, D. H., 111
London, Jack, 72
Lorenz, Konrad Z., 17
Mannix, Daniel P., 10
Maxwell, Gavin, 38
Melville, Herman, 75
Michener, James, 153
Read, Herbert, 90
Rourke, Constance, 67
Ryan, Cornelius, 60
Saroyan, William, 121
Silverberg, Robert, 89
Steinbeck, John, 104
Stuart, Jesse, 96
Teale, Edwin Way, 42
White, Stewart Edward, 138
Zim, Herbert S., 19

Index of Writing Skills

Adjectives, use of, 63–66, 84, 92, 118

Adverbs, use of, 72–78, 118–19

Choosing words, 57–78
  in description, 78, 86, 90, 92, 98
  in exposition, 145, 155
  in narration, 117–19
  for precise meanings, 57–78
    adjectives, 63–66
    adverbs, 72–78
    nouns, 57–62
    verbs, 67–71

Chronological order
  in explaining a process, 140
  of narratives in exposition, 151
  in paragraphs, 48–49

Coherence in paragraphs, 48–54
  through arrangement of details
    in chronological order, 48–50
    in order of importance, 50–52
    in order of location, 52–54
  through transitional expressions, 49–54

Description, 81–99
  arranging details in order of location, 52–54
  defined, 81
  in exposition, 143–46
  in narration, 111–20
  selection of details, 82, 86–87
  sensory details in, 95–99
  showing the location of details, 88–94
  specific details in, 81–87
  word choice in, 86–87, 90, 92, 98

Details
  arrangement of, in paragraphs, 48–54
    chronological order, 48–50
    order of importance, 50–52
    order of location, 52–54
  descriptive
    in exposition, 143–46
    in narration, 111–20
    in paragraphs, 49–54
    selection of, 81, 84–87
    showing the location of, 88–94
    using sensory, 95–99
    using specific, 81–87
  in paragraph development, 41–47
    examples, 41–43
    incident, 44–45
    reasons, 45–47

Dialogue, in narration, 121–29
  defined, 121
  dialogue tags, 127

Examples, developing paragraphs with, 41–43

Experience
as a source of ideas, 10–16
writing about, in narration, 103–29

Exposition, 133–56
defined, 133
description in, 143–46
developing a topic, 133–37
explaining a process, 138–42
narration in, 147–52
organization in, 133–37, 138–42, 147–52
supporting an opinion, 153–56
transitional expressions in, 135, 141, 151
unity in, 136
word choice in, 145, 155

Ideas, finding, 3–26
experience, 10–16
interests, 17–21
opinions, 22–27
people and places, 3–9

Incident
developing paragraphs with, 44–45
in exposition, 147–52

Interests, as a source of ideas, 17–21

Narration, 102–29
conclusion of, 108
defined, 103
description in, 111–20
development of, 108
dialogue in, 121–29
in exposition, 147–52
introduction of, 108
word choice in, 117–19

Nouns, use of, 57–62, 84, 117–18, 145

Opinion
as a source of ideas, 22–27
supporting, in a composition, 153–56

Order of importance, in paragraphs, 50–52

Order of location
in description, 88–94
in paragraphs, 52–54

Organization
in description, 88–94
in exposition, 133–37, 138–42
of narratives in exposition, 140, 147–52
in paragraphs, 48–54

Paragraphs, 31–54
arrangement of details in, 48–54
chronological order, 48–49
order of importance, 50–52
order of location, 52–54
coherence in, 48–54
development of, 41–47
with examples, 41–43
with an incident, 44–45
with reasons, 45–47
topic sentences in, 31–35
transitional expressions in, 49–50
unity in, 36–40

People and places, as a source of ideas, 3–9

Process, explanation of a, 138–42
chronological order in, 140
transitional expressions in, 141

Reasons
  developing paragraphs with, 45–47
  supporting an opinion with, 22–27, 153–56

Sensory details, use of, 95–99, 118

Supporting an opinion, 153–56

Topic, developing a
  in exposition, 133–37, 143–46, 147–52
  in paragraphs, 41–47

Topic sentences, 31–35

Transitional expressions
  coherence through, 49–50, 53–54
  defined, 49
  in description, 88–94
  in exposition, 135, 141
  with narratives in exposition, 151

Unity
  in exposition, 136
  in paragraphs, 36–40

Verbs, use of, 67–71, 98, 117, 155

Word choice, *see* Choosing words

5
6
7
8
9